Central Banking 101

Joseph Wang

New York, 2020

Joseph Wang

Contents

Joseph Wang

Preface

I dreamed of working in the financial markets. Unfortunately, I did not have that dream until after I graduated from Columbia Law School on the eve of the great financial crisis. While I sat in my office re-reading a 200-page loan agreement for the fourth time, I was aware that the world around me was changing. The Dow was gyrating a few percentage points a day, major financial institutions were teetering on collapse, and the Fed was printing money in a way it had never done before. I didn't understand much of what was going on, but it was exciting. I wanted to understand how it all worked.

I applied to over a hundred jobs in the financial markets, but the post-crisis world was not the best time to join the finance industry. Every job posting was flooded with resumes from newly laid-off bankers and traders (and a fair number of lawyers desperate to escape their tedious careers). Ultimately, I made my transition into the financial services by going back to school for a master's in economics at Oxford University. I had fortunately studied math and economics in college, so the shift was manageable. After a stint as a credit analyst, I landed a role as a trader on the Open Markets Desk of the New York Fed.

My time on the Desk offered me a glimpse behind the curtain as to how the financial system really worked. This is because the Desk has two very important responsibilities: gathering market intelligence for policy makers and executing open market operations.

Gathering market intelligence means having candid conversations with market participants on how they are viewing the market. The Desk regularly speaks with virtually every major market participant, from prominent investment banks to Fortune 500 corporate treasurers to large hedge funds. In addition, the Desk itself has access to extensive volumes of confidential data the Fed collects through its regulatory powers. The qualitative discussions and hard data give the Desk a substantial edge in understanding financial markets.

Executing open market operations means implementing the monetary policies decided by the Federal Open Markets Committee, such as large-scale asset purchases and FX-swap operations. The financial panics in 2008 and 2020 that swept through global markets were only stabilized when the Desk stepped up its operations. Open market operations basically mean printing money, sometimes a lot of money.

I took full advantage of my time on the Desk to learn as much as I could about the monetary system and the broader financial system. I often noticed that many people, even seasoned professionals, did not have a very strong understanding of how the monetary system worked. For example, the Fed's first foray into quantitative easing in 2008 sent the professional investment community into a frenzy. Gold prices skyrocketed to all-time highs as investors anticipated imminent hyperinflation, but not even mild inflation materialized.

The misunderstanding is understandable, as central banking is very complicated. There is a lot of conflicting information, even from purported experts. Without my time on the Desk, I would still be very fuzzy on many aspects of how the monetary system works. I remember sitting in my law office being intensely interested in understanding quantitative easing and what the Fed was doing, but forced to piece things together based on articles and blog posts by people that appeared to be credible. I couldn't find better resources.

Central Banking 101 is aimed at teaching the foundational aspects of central banking, as well as offering an overview of the financial markets. While intended as a broad introduction, it also includes special highlighted sections that offer deeper insight for more knowledgeable readers. Central Banking 101 is the book that I wish I had been able to read when I first began my journey in understanding the monetary system and the broader financial system.

I hope you find it interesting and helpful.

Note, the views I express are my own and do not necessarily reflect those of the Federal Reserve Bank of New York or the Federal Reserve System.

Joseph Wang

Section I Money and Banking

Chapter 1 – Types of Money

What is money? When most people think of money, they picture rectangular pieces of government-printed paper, known as fiat currency, decorated with historical figures. Although this is the most well-known form of money, it is only a small part of what constitutes money in the modern financial system. Look in your wallet and think about your day—how much currency do you carry and use? If you are like most people, then your salary is wired into your bank account and spent via electronic payments. The numbers that you see in a bank account are called bank deposits, a separate type of money that is created by commercial banks, not the government. Bank deposits are the vast majority of what the public thinks of as money.

In practice, bank deposits can be seamlessly converted into government-issued fiat currencies in real time at any bank or ATM machine. But the two are very different. A bank deposit is an "IOU" from a bank that can become worthless if the issuing bank goes bankrupt. On the other hand, a $100 dollar bill is issued by the Federal Reserve, which is part of the U.S. government. That $100 bill will have value as long as the United States exists. There is much more money in bank deposits than there is in paper bills, so in theory, a bank would run out of cash if everyone withdrew their deposits. But that's not really an issue because people today feel safe holding bank deposits, in part because the government provides $250,000 in FDIC deposit insurance for account holders. This makes bank deposits as safe as fiat currency for most people.

The third type of money is central bank reserves, a special type of money issued by the Federal Reserve that only commercial banks can hold.[1] Much like a customer's bank deposit is an "IOU" from a commercial bank, a central bank reserve is an "IOU" from the Federal Reserve. From a commercial bank's standpoint, currency and bank reserves are interchangeable. A commercial bank can convert its bank reserves to fiat currency by calling up the Federal Reserve and asking for a shipment of currency. A $1000 shipment of currency would be paid for by a $1000 decline in reserves from its account at the Fed. Commercial banks use bank reserves when they pay each other or anyone else who also has a Fed account, and they use currency or bank deposits to pay everyone else.

The final type of money is Treasuries, which is basically a type of money that also pays interest. Just like fiat

---

[1] The vast majority of reserves are held by commercial banks, but a select group of other institutions are also eligible to have reserve accounts at the Fed. These include government-sponsored enterprises (GSEs) like Fannie Mae, clearing houses like CME, credit unions, and the U.S. Treasury.

currencies and central bank reserves, Treasuries are issued by the U.S. government. They can be readily convertible to bank deposits by selling them in the market
or by using them as collateral for a loan. Imagine that
you are a large institutional investor or very wealthy
person with hundreds of millions of dollars. You are not
eligible to hold central bank reserves because you are
not a bank, it would not make sense for you to deposit
all that money at a commercial bank because it far exceeds FDIC insurance limits, and it would be silly to
hold a mountain of fiat currency at home. For you,
Treasuries are money.

Type of Money	Who Issues it	Who Can Hold	Size
Fiat currency	U.S. government	Everyone	$2 trillion
Bank deposits	Commercial banks	Everyone	$15.5 trillion domestically
Central bank reserves	U.S. government	Commercial banks	$3 trillion
Treasury securities	U.S. government	Everyone	$20 trillion
Sources: Federal Reserve H8 and U.S. Treasury as of June 2020			

In a functional financial system, all forms of money are
freely convertible to each other. When that conversion
breaks down, then serious problems in the financial
system emerge. In the following sections, we will discuss each type of money and provide illustrations of
what happens when their convertibility is impaired.

Quick Primer on Balance Sheet Accounting

A balance sheet gives an overview of a bank's assets and liabilities. It is written in double-entry bookkeeping fashion, so every asset is counterbalanced by a liability. This shows how assets are financed. Assets are instruments owned by the bank such as loans or securities that generate cash flow. Liabilities are what the bank needs to pay back, such as deposits or debt. At the end of the day, total assets must equal total liabilities plus equity. This means that a bank's assets are either funded by the owners (equity) or borrowings from others (liabilities).

A balance sheet is a good way to understand how a bank works. Every bank starts out with equity put up by investors on the liability side, and central bank reserves and currency on the asset side. From there, a bank expands its balance sheet by adding assets and paying for them by creating deposit liabilities. For example, a bank could make a business loan for $1000. This would lead to a $1000 loan asset, and a $1000 deposit liability. The bank simply adds $1000 in deposits to the borrowers account through a computer. We will discuss how money creation works more detail in the next chapter.

Commercial Bank Balance Sheet

Assets	Liabilities
Reserves	Equity
+ $1000 loan	+$1000 deposits

The same balance sheet principles apply to a central bank. When the Fed buys Treasuries or other assets, it pays for them by creating reserves.

Central Bank Reserves

Central bank reserves are created when the central bank buys financial assets or makes loans. The central bank is the only entity that can create central bank reserves, so the total amount of reserves in the financial system is completely determined by central bank actions.[2] For example, when the Federal Reserve purchases $1 billion in U.S. Treasury securities, it creates $1 billion in central bank reserves to pay for them. That happens whether the seller of the Treasuries is a commercial bank or a nonbank. If the Fed bought the Treasury security from a commercial bank, then the commercial bank's Treasury security asset is exchanged for central bank reserves.

Commercial Bank Sells Treasuries to Fed

Commercial Bank's balance sheet

Assets	Liabilities
- $1b Treasuries + $1b Reserves	

Corporation Sells Treasuries to Fed

Commercial Bank's balance sheet

Assets	Liabilities
+ $1b Reserves	+ $1b deposits to Corp.

---

[2] A commercial bank can convert its central bank reserves to fiat currency, which would reduce central bank reserves and increase currency outstanding. But in practice, this is not a meaningful level of activity since the bulk of transactions today are electronic and do not involve fiat currency.

Corporation's balance sheet

Assets	Liabilities
- $1b Treasuries	
+ $1b Bank deposits	

If the Fed purchased the Treasury security from some-one who is not a commercial bank, the situation is slightly different because they do not have a Fed account and are thus ineligible to hold central bank reserves. If a corporation sold $1 billion in Treasury securities to the Fed, then the sale proceeds would be deposited at the commercial bank that the corporation banks with. The Fed would add $1 billion in reserves to the commercial bank's Fed account, and the commercial bank would add $1 billion to the corporation's bank account. At the end of the transaction, the commercial bank would have a $1 billion in central bank reserves assets, balanced by an increase in $1 billion in bank deposit liabilities to the corporation.

Central bank reserves never leave the Fed's balance sheet, but they get shuffled around daily as commercial banks settle payments with each other. Suppose the corporation took half of that $1 billion and made a payment to its supplier who banked with a different bank. The corporation would see a $500 million decline in its bank account balance, while its supplier would see a $500 million increase in its bank account balance. Behind the scenes, the corporation's bank would send $500 million in central bank reserves to the supplier's bank, who would then credit the supplier's account with $500 million in bank deposits.

Corporation Pays $500 mil to Supplier

Corporation's Bank's Balance Sheet

Assets	Liabilities
$1b Reserves - $500 mil Reserves sent to Supplier's Bank	$1b deposits to Corp. - $500 mil deposits to Corp.

Corporation's Balance Sheet

Assets	Liabilities
$1b Bank deposits - $500 mil Bank deposits + $500 mil Supplies	

Supplier's Bank's Balance Sheet

Assets	Liabilities
+ $500 mil Reserves from Corporation's bank	+ $500 mil deposits to Supplier

Supplier's Balance Sheet

Assets	Liabilities
- $500 mil Supplies sold to Corporation + $500 mil Bank deposits	

Prior to the 2008 Financial Crisis, the Fed conducted monetary policy under a reserve scarcity regime where the Fed controlled short-term interest rates by making slight adjustments to the level of reserves in the banking system. There were only around $30 billion in reserves in the entire banking system, compared to a few trillion today. The level of reserves increased significantly as the Fed created reserves to pay for its quantitative easing program, in which they attempt to influence longer-term rates by buying longer-dated Treasuries. The Fed now controls short-term interest rates by adjusting the interest it pays banks on excess reserves and the offering rate of the Overnight Reverse Repo Facility,[3] a program where participants can loan money to the Fed. The Fed's operating framework is described in later sections.

How to Analyze Fed Reserves

Central bank reserves data are released in the weekly H.4.1 on the Fed's website. Below is a snapshot of the table that details reserve balances.

1. Factors Affecting Reserve Balances of Depository Institutions (continued) Millions of dollars				
Reserve Bank credit, related items, and reserve balances of depository institutions at Federal Reserve Banks	Averages of daily figures			Wednesday
	Week ended Jan 15, 2020	Change from week ended Jan 8, 2020	Jan 16, 2019	Jan 15, 2020
Currency in circulation (11)	1,797,265	- 7,742	+ 90,512	1,795,725
Reverse repurchase agreements (12)	266,447	- 12,004	+ 4,214	260,913
Foreign official and international accounts	265,788	- 9,498	+ 5,383	260,238
Others	659	- 2,506	- 1,170	675
Treasury cash holdings	177	+ 5	- 46	189
Deposits with F.R. Banks, other than reserve balances	424,014	- 10,541	- 735	449,695
Term deposits held by depository institutions	0	0	0	0
U.S. Treasury, General Account	350,987	- 16,015	- 193	380,802
Foreign official	5,182	0	- 65	5,181
Other (13)	67,846	+ 5,475	- 476	63,712
Other liabilities and capital (14)	45,028	+ 1,860	+ 60	44,241
Total factors, other than reserve balances, absorbing reserve funds	2,532,931	- 28,423	+ 94,004	2,550,762
Reserve balances with Federal Reserve Banks	1,686,801	+ 32,715	+ 22,663	1,673,362

The data shows the aggregate distribution of reserves among major reserve holder types. Focusing on the first column, which shows weekly averages as of January 15, 2020, you'll first note that currency in circulation is $1.79 trillion. That's the cumulative amount of reserves that have been converted to currency. When

---

[3] Repo loans, or repurchase agreements, are described in Chapter 6.

commercial banks need currency, they send central bank reserves to the Fed, who sends over an armored car with currency. The reserves are essentially extinguished and replaced with currency.

The next large item is the $265 billion in foreign official and international accounts. That is the Foreign Repo pool, which is like a checking account for foreign central banks. Foreign central banks have the option of depositing their dollars at the New York Fed, but the transaction is structured as a secured repo loan. The foreign central bank does not hold reserves (it holds a repo loan, where it is lending money to the Fed), but when it moves money out of commercial banks into the Foreign Repo pool, then reserves leave the banking system into a separate Foreign Repo Facility account.

The next largest item at $350 billion is the Treasury General Account (TGA), which is the U.S. Treasury's checking account. When payments are made to the U.S. Treasury, such as tax payments, reserves leave the commercial banking system and enter into the TGA. The $67.8 billion under "Other" are the reserve balances of GSEs like Fannie Mae and Designated Financial Market Utilities like the CME Clearing House. Finally, at the very bottom is the level of reserves held by commercial banks: $1.68 trillion.

Bank Deposits

Bank deposits are created when a commercial bank creates a loan or when it buys a financial asset. A common misconception is that a bank takes in deposits and then lends those deposits out to other people. Rather than lend out deposits, a bank simply creates bank deposits out of thin air when it makes a loan.[4] This is very similar to the way a central bank acts when it creates central bank reserves. The central bank acts as a bank to commercial banks, and commercial banks act as a bank to nonbanks like individuals and corporations.

However, a meaningful difference is that there are many commercial banks while there is only one central bank. As there is only one central bank, all the reserves created stay on the central bank's balance sheet and are shuffled among the different reserve accounts as commercial banks make payments to each other. In the case of commercial banks, each commercial bank has its own balance sheet and creates its own deposits. Therefore, it is possible for a depositor to withdraw a bank deposit and move it off one commercial bank's balance sheet onto another commercial bank's balance sheet. When this happens, one commercial bank must make a payment to another. This payment is made in the form of central bank reserves.

Since commercial banks create deposits out of thin air, they will have many more deposits than central bank reserves. In practice, a commercial bank both receives and makes large volumes of payments each day. At the end of the day, the amount of reserves they have usually

---

[4] For more details, see McLeay, Michael, Amar Radia, and Ryland Thomas. "Money Creation in the Modern Economy." Quarterly Bulletin. Bank of England, Q1 2014.

doesn't change that much, so they only need to hold a small amount of reserves against the deposits they create. This is known as fractional reserve banking. Should the commercial bank have more outflows than anticipated, it can always borrow reserves from another commercial bank or from the Fed to make payments.

While bank deposits are the most common form of money, they are also the least secure. They are created by the private sector, so they are not risk-free. Banking crises occur when a bank has made too many bad loans and becomes insolvent. When that happens, a bank's deposits may no longer be convertible to currency at par, so a $100 deposit may not be convertible to $100 in currency as depositors share in the loan losses. Depositors will panic and try to withdraw their deposits at the same time, accelerating the bank's demise. During the wildcat banking days of the nineteenth century, there was no unified currency, so each individual commercial bank created its own deposits and printed its own bank note currency. Bank collapses were so frequent then that the bank notes each bank created were only accepted at discounts to face value to account for default risk.

Since then, the U.S. government has made many advancements to reduce the risk of banking crisis, including bank deposit guarantees, stronger bank regulation, and emergency loans offered to banks via the Federal Reserve discount window. Together, these measures essentially work to make bank deposits more risk-free and "money-like," comparable to central bank reserves or currency. In practice, the $250,000 FDIC deposit guarantee fully covers the deposit balances of the vast majority of depositors. For these people, bank deposits are risk-free money.

Central Bank Digital Currency

Central Bank Digital Currencies (CBDC) are an increasingly popular topic in the central banking community, with almost all major central banks at least looking into the idea. A CBDC essentially allows everyone to have an account at the central bank. Instead of holding bank deposits at a commercial bank, the public would also have the option of holding something like reserves at the central bank. A CBDC would potentially replace both physical currency and bank deposit money.

The core benefits of a CBDC are being touted as security and efficiency. Instead of bearing the credit risk of commercial bank deposits, non-banks would be able to hold risk-free deposits at the central bank. Payments would be faster because everyone would have an account at the central bank so money would simply be shuffled between different CBDC accounts. There would be no need for inter-bank payments.

In practice, the purported benefits of CBDC are illusory. Government deposit insurance already makes bank deposits safe, and electronic payments today are already instant and very low cost. The true purpose of a CDBC is as a policy tool to conduct fiscal and monetary policy.

CBDCs would give the government virtually complete control over the monetary system. They would know exactly how much money everyone has and who they send it to. They could debit or credit money to anyone's CBDC account at will. They could lower or raise the interest rates of anyone's CBDC account at will. At the moment, all those powers belong to the private commercial banks.

In a CBDC world tax evasion and money laundering would be impossible, and the government would be able to manipulate spending by giving money directly to people. They could also directly take money away from people as a punishment. If their models suggested a negative 5% interest rate would stimulate the economy, then they could apply it instantly to everyone or even selectively to certain people with the click of a button. Governments love CBDCs because it significantly increases their power.

But from an individual's perspective, a CBDC would be a historic blow to privacy and individual liberty.

Treasuries

Treasury securities are unsecured debt issued by the federal government and are the dominant form of money in the financial system because they are safe, liquid, and widely accepted. Unlike bank deposits, they are risk-free because they are fully backed by the federal government. Unlike central bank reserves, they can be held by anyone. Unlike fiat currency, they pay interest and can be sent electronically throughout the world. While a retail investor would likely hold most of their money in the form of bank deposits, an institutional investor would use Treasury securities for this purpose. Treasury securities are essentially money for large investors.

Note that there is a difference in the degree of "moneyness" of Treasuries when compared to other types of money. $100 in bank deposits, $100 in central bank reserves, and $100 in currency will always have a nominal value of $100. However, a purchase of $100 worth of Treasury securities can fluctuate with market pricing. Longer-dated Treasuries are more sensitive to expected changes in inflation and interest rates, so their market values fluctuate the most, while the market value of shorter-dated Treasuries fluctuates very little. When held to maturity, these fluctuations in value do not matter, but if sold before maturity they could result in gains or losses.

Treasuries offer investors an easy way to store large amounts of money. Investors would not be able to use Treasuries to purchase groceries, but they can easily convert them to bank deposits by selling them or borrowing against them. The Treasury cash market and repo loan market is very liquid and operates around the clock in all of the world's financial centers. In practice, investors are not using their Treasuries to buy real economy items but to make other investments. To do so, investors can pledge Treasury securities as collateral at their broker to purchase financial assets. Essentially, an investor can buy financial assets like stocks or bonds using Treasury securities.

Treasury securities are how the U.S. Treasury creates money. When the U.S. Treasury issues $100 in Treasury securities to an investor, the investor exchanges $100 in bank deposits for $100 in Treasury securities. From the investor's perspective, they simply exchanged one form of money for another. From the Treasury's perspective, it is able to purchase goods and services from the real economy by paying with Treasury securities it created. Following the chain of payments can help illustrate that.

The investor will have $100 less in bank deposits after their purchase, and the investor's commercial bank will send the U.S. Treasury $100 in central bank reserves on the investor's behalf to settle the payment. Note that the U.S. Treasury has an account at the Fed, so it can also hold central bank reserves. When U.S. Treasury spends the $100 it borrowed, then that $100 in central bank reserves ends up back in the commercial banking system. For example, suppose the U.S. Treasury used the $100 to make a payment to a doctor for Medicare expenses. Then the doctor's commercial bank would receive $100 in central bank reserves from the U.S. Treasury and in turn add $100 in bank deposits in the doctor's bank account. At the end of the day, the amount of bank deposits and central bank reserves in the banking system is unchanged, but there is now an additional $100 in Treasury securities outstanding. The investor can take that $100 in Treasuries and use it to buy other financial assets, or they can sell it for bank deposits to buy real economy goods.

Treasury Issues $100 in Treasury Securities and then Spends the Money on Medicare Payments

Treasury's Balance Sheet

Assets	Liabilities
+$100 Reserves	+$100 Treasury debt
-$100 Reserves	-$100 Medicare payment

Banking System's Balance Sheet

Assets	Liabilities
-$100 Reserves to settle Treasury purchase	-$100 Investor's Deposits to purchase Treasuries
+ $100 Reserves to Medicare payment	+$100 Doctor's deposits for Medicare service

Investor's Balance Sheet

Assets	Liabilities
-$100 Bank deposits	
+$100 Treasuries	

Doctor's Balance Sheet

Assets	Liabilities
- $100 Receivables	
+ $100 Bank deposits	

In addition to Treasuries, there are other government-issued securities that have varying degrees of "money-ness." After Treasuries, the most liquid and safe assets are Agency RMBS. These are residential mortgage-backed securities (MBS) that are guaranteed by the government. While risk-free and actively traded, they are less liquid than Treasuries. The Fed prefers to conduct monetary policy by purchasing Treasuries, but they also actively purchase Agency MBS in their quantitative easing purchases.

When the Treasury Market Breaks

Investors throughout the world expect to be able to take their Treasuries and easily convert them into bank deposits that can then be used to make payments. This is comparable to the expectation everyone has of being able to go to the ATM and convert their bank deposits to currency. If one day all the ATMs were to display a "Not Available" sign, then the public would panic. That was essentially what happened in the Treasury market during the COVID-19 panic of March 2020.

In March 2020, people throughout the world were scared and they wanted to hold dollars. Investors were withdrawing from their investment funds, and foreigners were selling their home currency for U.S. dollars. To meet these withdrawals, investment funds and foreign central banks sold their Treasuries just as if they were withdrawing from an ATM. But in this case, they found that they could not sell their Treasuries except at sizable discounts. The ATM machine was broken.

When an institutional investor sells their securities, they call a dealer and expect the dealer to offer a price. The dealer would normally buy the security, hold on to it, and then sell it to another investor, earning the difference between the prices. In March of 2020, a large number of investors called up their dealers and asked to sell securities. Mortgage REITs, who borrow money to invest in mortgage securities, were selling large amounts of Agency MBS to repay those loans. Corporate bond ETFs were trying to sell their bonds to meet investor withdrawals. Prime money market funds were trying to sell their commercial paper holdings for the same reason. Dealers were suddenly flooded with securities and reaching the regulatory limits of their security inventory holdings.

In the 2008 Financial Crisis, there was a run on the dealers as investors refused to lend to dealers over concerns of their financial condition. This led dealers to liquidate their security holdings at fire sales prices to repay existing loans, aggravating the financial panic. In response to this, regulators introduced new rules which made it more difficult for dealers to hold large inventories of securities and more expensive to hold riskier securities. These regulations strengthened the financial position of dealers, but in March 2020, they hampered the dealers' ability to buy securities from their clients. The dealers reached their inventory limits and could not buy any more, even safe Treasury securities.

Investors were aware of the dislocations happening in financial markets but were surprised that they suddenly could not even sell Treasury securities. This led to a massive panic where anything that could be sold, was sold. All financial markets crashed. The markets did not calm down until the Fed intervened.

In recognition of the balance sheet limitations of dealers, the Fed did three things. First, the Fed gave bank holding companies a temporary reprieve of some of the regulations that limited their balance sheet size. Second, they opened up a new Foreign Repo Facility to allow foreign central banks to obtain dollars without selling their Treasury securities. Third, the Fed resumed massive quantitative easing. The last point was key in stabilizing the markets. In the brief span of a few weeks, the Fed purchased almost $2 trillion in Treasury securities and Agency MBS from the dealers. These purchases offered a way for dealers to off-load their large inventory of securities and have room again to purchase securities from their clients. This restored the "moneyness" of Treasury securities and significantly helped stabilize the broader market.

Fiat Currency

Though the term may be unfamiliar, fiat currency needs no introduction as it is the most visible form of money. Currency is printed and guaranteed by the government. A depositor can go to a commercial bank or ATM machine and convert their bank deposits into currency. Commercial banks in turn make sure their bank deposits are freely convertible to fiat currency by holding enough currency in their vaults. Commercial banks that need more can convert their central bank reserves into currency by calling the Fed. The Fed stands ready to send armored vehicles loaded with currency to meet commercial bank needs.

There is one significant advantage that currency holds over other forms of money—it is outside of the financial system. Like gold or silver, currency physically exists and is accepted as value regardless of who holds it. The government controls the everything in the financial system because it has power over the central bank and commercial banks. Someone on the wrong side of the law may not be able to access anything in the financial system, but would still be able to use the currency stashed beneath their mattress. All other forms of money are essentially just numbers on a computer screen. In fact, there is some evidence that a sizable amount of $100 bills are largely used as a store of value for people who wish avoid government scrutiny.

Most Currency is Actually Held Abroad

Despite the increasing popularity of electronic payments, the amount of currency in circulation has steadily increased over the years to around $20 trillion in 2020. Interestingly, the $100 dollar bill is the most common bill in circulation. There are 15 billion $100 bills in circulation, compared to 13 billion $1 bills and 11.5 billion $20 bills. From a dollar value perspective, around 80% of the $2 trillion in circulation is held in the form of $100 bills.

Despite the large number of $100 bills in circulation, most Americans rarely use or see a $100 bill in their day-to-day life. Instead, they frequently see and use $20 or smaller bills. Research suggests this is because most of the $100 bills are held abroad.[5]

---

[5] Judson, Ruth. "The Death of Cash? Not So Fast: Demand for U.S. Currency at Home and Abroad, 1990-2016." In *International Cash Conference 2017 – War on Cash: Is There a Future for Cash?* Deutsche Bundesbank, 2017. https://econpapers.repec.org/paper/zbwiccp17/162910.htm.

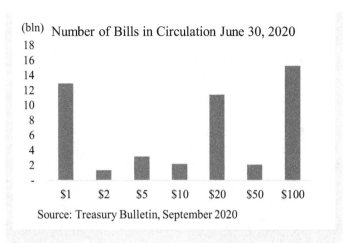

(bln) Number of Bills in Circulation June 30, 2020

Source: Treasury Bulletin, September 2020

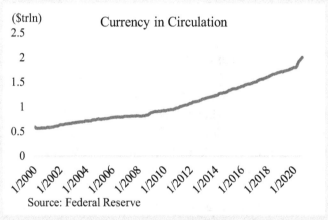

($trln) Currency in Circulation

Source: Federal Reserve

There are a few reasons why so much dollar currency is held abroad. Wealthy people in developing countries like Argentina often prefer to store part of their wealth in major currencies like the U.S. dollar. This is because developing countries are often poorly managed and have double-digit inflation rates. In fact, some developing countries like El Salvador completely cede their control of monetary policy and use the dollar as their official currency. In addition, criminals often hold their assets in the form of dollar currency because it is easily transportable and difficult to trace. Police raids on foreign drug cartels have at times uncovered hundreds of millions of dollar currency.

Globally, dollar currency is held internationally as a store of value, like gold during the gold-standard era. We currently live in a dollar-standard world, where the U.S. dollar is widely accepted throughout the world and perceived to be safe. This led to a boom in offshore dollar banking, but also in offshore demand for dollar currency.

Common Questions

This chapter aimed at providing a framework to understand today's monetary system. This framework should allow the reader to better understand the implications of central bank actions and dispel some of the most common misperceptions. Here are a few common questions to practice the application of the framework.

<u>Why don't banks lend out their reserves?</u>

When quantitative easing was first introduced, many market commentators saw the aggregate level of commercial bank reserves explode higher and wondered why banks were not "lending out their reserves." As discussed, central bank reserves can only be held by commercial banks and can never leave the Fed's balance sheet. The level of central bank reserves held by banks is determined by the Fed's actions and is unaffected by the amount of loans made by commercial banks. In fact, commercial banks are not constrained by reserves in their decision to make loans because they can always go out and borrow reserves.

The lending constraint for commercial banks is either regulatory or due to commercial conditions. Commercial banks are highly regulated by a myriad of rules that constrain the size of their balance, the quality of their assets, and the composition of their liabilities. These regulations make the banking system safer but also limit the amount of loans available. Commercial banks also are only interested in lending if they can make a profit, and profitable borrowers are harder to find during a recession when the likelihood of default is relatively high. That was the case in the aftermath of the 2008 Financial Crisis.

Will the stock market soar because of all the cash on the sidelines?

Sometimes commentators look at the level of deposits in the banking system and suggest that financial asset prices will explode when all that money is spent.

Just as the level of central bank reserves is determined by the Fed, so the level of bank deposits in the banking system is largely determined by the collective actions of commercial banks.[6] Bank deposits are created when a commercial bank purchases an asset or creates a loan,

---

[6] It is also in part determined by central bank actions, where increases in reserves also increase bank deposits.

and they are destroyed when the loan or asset is repaid. The level of bank deposits is thus largely an indicator of the level of loans made by the banking system.

When an investor purchases stocks or bonds with their bank deposits, then their bank deposit ends up in the bank account of whoever sold them the stock or the bond. The total level of the bank deposits in the banking system is unchanged. The bank deposits are essentially being shuffled around the commercial banking system, but they neither increase nor decrease. Large amounts of investment can occur at both low and high aggregate levels of bank deposits.

Chapter 2 – The Money Creators

In this chapter, we further describe the three creators of money: the Fed, commercial banks, and the Treasury.

The Fed

The Fed has a dual mandate: full employment and stable prices. In practice, the Fed doesn't know what unemployment rate corresponds to full employment and it hasn't been able to sustainably reach its 2% inflation target for over a decade. The Fed's experience with inflation is not unlike the experience of other major central banks such as the Bank of Japan (BOJ) and the European Central Bank (ECB), who have experimented boldly over the past decade but consistently failed to reach their inflation targets. The Fed's efforts to achieve its dual mandate has also led it to gradually expand its policy tool kit and engage in unconventional monetary policy, including large-scale money printing.

The Fed thinks of the economy through the lens of interest rates, which is the primary tool through which the Fed achieves its mandate.[7] In the eyes of the Fed, there is a thing called r* (pronounced "r star"), which is the neutral rate of interest at which the economy is neither expanding nor contracting. When interest rates are below r*, then the economy is expanding, inflation is rising, and unemployment is ticking lower. When interest rates are above r*, then the economy is slowing, inflation is declining, and unemployment is ticking higher. The Fed employs a small army of Ph.D. economists to determine what the level of r* is at the moment, as it changes over time, and then sets out to lower or raise interest rates to achieve its mandate. The Fed's money printing is used as part of its efforts to exert greater control over longer-term interest rates.

When the economy is in trouble and the Fed's models show that r* is currently a very low or even negative number, then the Fed will do everything it can to get interest rates below r* to promote economic growth. They will first cut their target overnight interest rate to zero, then they will try to lower longer-term interest rates by buying lots of longer-dated Treasury securities, which will then increase the price of the Treasury securities and correspondingly lower their yields. Longer-dated Treasury securities are less sensitive to changes in the overnight interest rate, so the Fed tries to indirectly influence them through quantitative easing.

---

[7] Powell, Jerome. "Monetary Policy in a Changing Economy." Speech, August 24, 2018. https://www.federalreserve.gov/newsevents/speech/powell20180824a.htm.

The Open Markets Desk

The Open Markets Desk ("the Desk") is the Fed's trading desk. It is primarily responsible for two things: executing open market operations, like quantitative easing, and collecting market intelligence.

The Desk collects market intelligence through a wide network of contacts. Their main contacts are the primary dealers, who are obligated to speak with the Desk as part of their primary dealer responsibilities. On a secondary basis, the Desk speaks with commercial banks, government-sponsored enterprises, hedge funds, pensions funds, corporate treasurers, and small dealers. Generally speaking, most significant players in the financial markets will have a relationship with the Desk. These secondary sources are not obligated to speak with the Desk like the primary dealers are, but they are generally happy to maintain a relationship with the Desk. They understand that the conversations are confidential and are happy to help the Fed carry out its work.

The market intelligence collected by the Desk is disseminated across the Federal Reserve system through brief research notes and daily products. Every day the Desk gives a daily morning call on developments in the financial markets based on what they have seen on Bloomberg and gathered from market contacts. The call is given in the Desk's briefing room, a large meeting room with a long wooden desk in the middle and seats along the walls. Fed officials throughout the Federal Reserve system are invited to dial in. In times of market stress, these calls are attended by Fed officials at the highest level. After the call, there is a question and answer segment where policy makers ask questions and subject matter experts sitting in the briefing room stand up to answer.

In addition to the daily briefings, Desk subject matter experts periodically publish research notes on developments in their area of expertise. These internally published notes are based on the Fed's confidential data and market intelligence.

With respect to operations, the Desk is organized by asset classes much like any other trading floor. The primary asset classes are Treasuries, Mortgages, and Money Markets. Within each team, traders operate in a rotational framework, where they have different operational responsibilities each week, and sometimes get a week off to focus on research pieces. This is in part to make sure everyone knows how to conduct each operation and in part to keep staff from getting too bored. One week, a trader could be running the Desk's reverse repo operation, and the next week, they could be waking up early to publish the Desk's benchmark reference rates.

When the Fed undertakes quantitative easing (QE) it will announce the quantity, pace, and type of assets it will purchase, but it does not know beforehand how the market will react. This is understandable, as market reactions are very difficult to predict because it is not clear what is already priced into the market. The Fed will size its program based on internal models and try to determine the market's expectations using surveys of a wide range of market participants. The Fed will then adjust the program on an ongoing basis, mindful of potential side effects such as buying so much of a specific security that normal market functioning is impaired.

When the Fed purchases a financial asset, it pays for it by creating bank reserves. Nonbanks cannot hold reserves because they do not have an account at the Fed. When the Fed purchases a financial asset from a nonbank investor, the Fed sends the payment as reserves to the investor's commercial bank. The commercial bank then credits the investor's bank account. In this instance, the commercial bank is acting as an intermediary between the Fed and the investor since the investor is unable to hold reserves. The Fed's action of purchasing assets increases the level of central bank reserves in the system as well as commercial bank deposits.

The Fed's goal with QE is to lower longer-term interest rates, with the increase in reserves and bank deposits being a necessary byproduct. Academic models suggest that QE is effective in lowering interest rates and does help boost inflation.[8] However, the experience of the Fed, the BOJ, and the ECB all show that massive QE, at least by itself, is not enough to sustainably move inflation higher. All three major central banks have had

---

[8] Engen, Eric, Thomas Laubach, and Dave Reifschneider. "The Macroeconomic Effects of the Federal Reserve's Unconventional Monetary Policies." Finance and Economics Discussion Series 2015-005. Washington: Board of Governors of the Federal Reserve System, 2015. http://dx.doi.org/10.17016/FEDS.2015.005.

trouble reaching their inflation mandates for over a decade but continue to believe in the utility of QE.

QE appears to lift financial asset prices but not necessarily economic activity. QE essentially converts Treasuries into bank deposits and reserves, thus forcing commercial banks as a whole to hold more of their money in the form of central bank reserves, and it forces nonbanks as a whole to hold more of their money in the form of bank deposits. Inflation occurs when demand in the economy pushes against supply, and money that was held in Treasuries was money that likely wasn't going to be spent in the real economy. Forced to trade in their Treasuries for bank deposits, nonbanks can trade their bank deposits for higher-yielding corporate debt or speculate on equity investments. Banks, who have more limited investment options due to regulation, may trade their reserves for higher-yielding Agency MBS. The portfolio rebalancing among nonbanks and banks pushes asset prices higher.

There does not appear to be a limit to the amount of quantitative easing a central bank can do. While the Fed has purchased a few trillion in assets, that is only a fraction of U.S. GDP. The BOJ has purchased assets amounting to over 100% of Japan's GDP, and there does not yet appear to be any signs of financial instability or currency weakness. However, the BOJ's large government bond holdings have effectively destroyed the Japanese bond market. Rather than reflect underlying economic conditions, the Japanese bond market appears to reflect only the dictates of Japanese policy makers. On some days, no Japanese government bonds are traded at all.[9]

Central Banker Community

The international central banking community is surprisingly tight-knit, with frequent meetings and even staff exchanges occurring on an ongoing basis. Of course, this is limited to countries on friendly terms. On the Desk there is always a secondee from each of major central banks—the ECB, BOJ, and BOE—and often other smaller central banks. These secondees join the Desk on a temporary basis for one to two years, during which they are given the same responsibilities and security clearances as American staff. They are universally top-notch in their abilities and very pleasant to work with. They usually receive a significant promotion upon return to their home central bank.

On a more formal basis, there are monthly conference calls with a number of central banks on developments in financial markets. Usually the calls are attended by the BOJ, Bank of England (BOE), ECB, Swiss National Bank (SNB), and Bank of Canada (BOC). During the conference calls, staff at each respective bank provide a very brief update on developments in their home financial markets and are available to take questions. The Desk has a particularly close relationship with BOJ,

---

[9] Anstey, Chris, and Hidenori Yamanaka. "Not a Single Japanese 10-Year Bond Traded Tuesday." *Bloomberg*, March 13, 2018. https://www.bloomberg.com/news/articles/2018-03-14/not-a-single-japanese-10-year-bond-traded-tuesday-death-by-boj.

where staff from the BOJ are welcome to meet daily for discussions on market developments.

The Desk also has formal high-level meetings periodically with the ECB and BOJ. These meetings are held on a rotating basis in Tokyo, Frankfurt, and New York.

The Commercial Banks

A commercial bank is a special type of business that holds a license from the government to create money. Almost all the money the general public uses is created by commercial banks. The ability to create money makes these banks an indispensable part the economy; when they create more money, there is more economic growth. The basic business model of a commercial bank is earning the difference in interest rates between the assets it holds and the liabilities it owes. The assets a commercial bank holds are typically loans that it originated, including mortgage, commercial, and consumer loans. Commercial banks also typically hold high-quality securities like Treasuries or Agency MBS as investments.

On the liability side, the bulk of commercial bank liabilities are retail deposits, which are bank deposits owed to individuals. Other liabilities include wholesale deposits, which are deposits owed to institutional investors like money market funds. Retail deposits earn little interest, while wholesale deposits tend to earn market-rate interest. This is because retail depositors tend to be less sensitive to interest rates, which means that retail investors keep their deposits at a bank even if they are earning no interest. In contrast, institutional investors are very interest-rate sensitive and are willing to withdraw their deposits to earn slightly higher interest rates elsewhere. Commercial banks prefer to have more retail deposits because those lower their interest-rate costs and are more stable. Institutional investors tend to withdraw their deposits at the first sign of trouble in the markets, leaving commercial banks that relied on those deposits scrambling for funding.

Commercial banking sounds like a great business where you can make loans, create deposits, and watch the interest income roll in. There is still some work underneath this to make sure things go smoothly. A commercial bank faces two fundamental problems: solvency and liquidity. Solvency is making sure the bank deposits it creates are backed by sound loans, and liquidity is making sure those deposits are freely convertible to bank deposits created by other commercial banks and to fiat currency.

In the best scenario, a commercial bank makes a loan to a borrower, who then dutifully pays back the interest and principal of the loan. In our fractional reserve banking system, a commercial bank only needs about $5 of its own money to create $100 in loans and deposits. When business goes well, the owners of the bank can earn interest on $100 of loans even if they only invested $5. But if the borrower defaults on the loan, then the commercial bank must take a loss. In this example, if $5 worth of loans are defaulted on and written off, then the commercial bank is insolvent and may have to file for bankruptcy.

The highly leveraged nature of a commercial bank means they have the potential to earn lots of money but also to bankrupt themselves rapidly. It's no surprise to see that banking crises have erupted frequently throughout history. As a result, commercial banks must be very careful when making loans. They make sure that the borrower is creditworthy by studying the borrowers' financial situation and purpose for borrowing, and they often seek additional guarantees or collateral. For example, mortgage loans are secured by the house being purchased. In the event of default, the bank can take the house and sell it to satisfy the loan.

The second problem a commercial bank must solve is liquidity. Suppose that the bank makes a $100 loan to a creditworthy borrower, but then the borrower immediately withdraws the money to pay their supplier, who banks with another commercial bank. Commercial banks have to make sure they have enough central bank reserves to settle payments with other commercial banks and that they have enough currency on hand to meet any depositor withdrawals. This can be a problem for a commercial bank that has little reserves or currency on hand and whose assets are illiquid, meaning they cannot easily be sold. A bank that cannot meet payments or withdrawals will likely panic its depositors even if it is fundamentally sound.

To solve liquidity problems, commercial banks carefully study the daily payments needs of their customers and then seek to hold enough liquid assets to meet those needs. These assets are usually central bank reserves, but they can also be Treasury securities or Agency residential MBS (RMBS). If a bank underestimated its liquidity, it can still go borrow from another commercial bank or an institutional investor. As a last resort, a commercial bank can borrow from the Fed's discount window. There is a strong stigma associated with this last option because it suggests the bank is in such dire straits that no one in the private sector would lend to them. Discount-window borrowing is the absolute last resort of any commercial bank.

Here is an example of how payments would work in two scenarios: a world with only one bank and a world with two banks.

I.   A world with only one bank

Alpha Bank's Balance Sheet

Assets	Liabilities
Reserves	Equity
+ $1 mill loan to John	+ $1 mill deposits to John
	- $1 mill sent to Tim
	+ $1 mill deposits to Tim

Suppose there is only one bank in the entire world, Alpha Bank. John the farmer goes to Alpha Bank and asks for a loan of $1 million so that he can pay Tim the lumberjack for some lumber. Alpha Bank looks over John's financials, decides he is a good credit risk, and then grants the loan. With a few keystrokes, Alpha Bank puts $1 million into John's bank account. John logs into his bank account, sees the $1 million, and then sends it to Tim. Since Alpha Bank is the only bank in the world, Alpha Bank simply goes onto its computer and moves that $1 million from John's account to Tim's account. Liquidity problems do not exist in a world with only one bank because everything is done on the bank's balance sheet.

II.   A world with two banks

Suppose that this time there are two banks in the world, Alpha Bank and Zed Bank. This time, John the farmer banks with Alpha Bank, but Tim the lumberjack banks with Zed Bank. After Alpha Bank makes the loan, John logs into his account and requests the $1 million be sent to Tim's account at Zed Bank. In this case, Alpha Bank can no longer simply shuffle numbers on its books but will have to send a payment to Zed Bank. Alpha Bank does this by sending $1 million in central bank reserves to Zed Bank, which receives the payment and adds $1 million into Tim's account.

Alpha Bank's Balance Sheet

Assets	Liabilities
Reserves + $1 mill loan to John - $1 mill reserves to Zed Bank	Equity + $1 mill deposits to John - $1 mill John sent to Tim

Zed Bank's Balance Sheet

Assets	Liabilities
Reserves + $1 mil reserves from Alpha Bank	Equity + $1 mill deposits to Tim

If Alpha Bank does not have enough bank reserves to make this payment, it will have to borrow the reserves. Alpha Bank can borrow central bank reserves from Zed Bank and then send them right back as payment on behalf of Tim. Alpha Bank can also borrow from the Fed's discount window as a last resort. Note that Alpha Bank can also borrow from nonbanks like money market funds, even though nonbanks cannot hold central bank reserves. This is because the nonbank's bank will have to send reserves to Alpha Bank to settle the loan proceeds. Alpha Bank would book a deposit liability to the nonbank, balanced by central bank reserves as an asset.

Limits on Credit Creation

It sounds like commercial banks are magic money trees, but there are limits to the amount of money they can create. These limits come through regulation and profitability. Since banks are historically prone to banking crises, they are heavily regulated. In addition to frequent regulatory reporting, the very largest banks even have regulators that sit on-site at the bank, supervising their daily actions. One of the regulations is a leverage ratio, which constrains the size of a bank's balance sheet for a given level of loss-absorbing capital. For example, under a 20x leverage ratio rule, a bank with $5 of capital can only have $100 worth of assets. The leverage ratio is designed to make sure a bank holds enough capital to absorb potential losses. Another important regulation is a capital ratio, which requires banks to hold a level of capital in line with the riskiness of their investments. For example, a bank with a portfolio full of corporate loans would be required to hold more capital than a bank with a portfolio full of Treasuries.

In a broader sense, commercial bank money creation is limited by the investment opportunities available. The equity investors in a bank want to earn a high return on their investment, so they want the bank to make investments that earn higher interest income. When the economy is booming, many borrowers are willing to pay high interest rates to fund profitable projects, but in a recession, there are far fewer worthwhile opportunities. Banks thus create more money during economic booms. During a recession, a bank may contract its lending, naturally reducing the supply of money as the economy has a lower demand for money.

How to Study Banks

A wide range of data on bank balance sheets is publicly available and can help you understand what is going on in the banking system. On an individual bank level, U.S. banks publicly report detailed balance sheet data each quarter on their call reports to the Federal Financial Institutions Examination Council (FFIEC) (Form FFIEC 031/041/02). On a national banking-system level, the Federal Reserve reports aggregated data each week through their H.8 data release. On a global banking-system level, the Bank of International Settlements (BIS) reports aggregated data each quarter in their International Banking Statistics.

Call Reports. The call reports are regulatory filings that all U.S. commercial banks and U.S. branch offices of foreign banks are required to file quarterly. They offer quarter-end snapshots of the balance sheets of banks, including the types of loans and securities they invest in and the types of deposits they rely on. The filings are detailed and most useful to an analyst who is trying to figure out if a particular bank is a good investment. From the report, an analyst can have a sense of the business model of a bank and how risky it is. The reports are publicly available on the FFIEC's website about 6 weeks after each quarter-end.

Weekly H.8. The H.8, titled "Assets and Liabilities of Commercial Banks in the United States," is a weekly publication produced by the Federal Reserve that provides aggregated balance sheet data of commercial banks located in the U.S. The data is not as detailed as the call reports but is produced more often and is useful for any analyst studying macroeconomic trends. For example, during the 2020 COVID-19 crisis, many corporations were reportedly hoarding cash amidst high degrees of economic uncertainty. Their actions could be clearly seen in the H.8, where a large spike in commercial loans showed that corporations were drawing down their revolving loans for extra cash. The H.8 also clearly illustrated a surge in aggregate banking sector reserves that reflected the Fed's aggressive asset purchases, and a decline in consumer credit as consumers retrenched amidst record high unemployment.

International Banking Data. The BIS collects data from central banks throughout the world and publishes aggregated data that shows how the banking system is structured on an international level. It publishes two sets of banking statistics: Locational Banking Statistics (LBS) and Consolidated Banking Statistics (CBS). The two sets of data complement each other in that the LBS shows the activity of banks within a reporting country vis-à-vis residents in other countries, while the CBS shows the activity of banks by nationality and their activity vis-à-vis residents in other countries. For example, the LBS can tell you the level of liabilities banks located in the U.S. have to residents in France. This would include the liabilities of U.S. branch offices of French banks, because the branch offices are located in the U.S. The CBS could tell you amount of liabilities American banks have to residents in France, excluding the liabilities of U.S. branch offices of French banks. The International Banking Data is very high level and most useful for a macro analyst trying to understand the global financial system. Indeed, the offshore dollar banking system can only be understood through the BIS data.

In practice, the public sector will have much better data on commercial banks than anything the private sector sees. Regulations enacted in the aftermath of the 2008 Financial Crisis gave the Federal Reserve and other regulators enormous power to collect very detailed data at a high frequency, even daily in the case of the largest banks. This makes banking crises like those of 2008 highly unlikely. Instability usually arises in corners of the market the regulators are unaware of; today, those corners are the shadow banking sector, which we will cover in the next chapter.

The Treasury

The Treasury Department is the part of the U.S. government that collects taxes and issues Treasury securities. The Treasury does not decide how much debt to issue; that is determined by the federal government's deficit, which is a result of decisions by Congress. Congress enacts legislation that determines the federal government's spending and its tax revenues, the difference of which is the deficit.

However, the Treasury does decide how it will go about funding the deficit. This gives Treasury influence over the shape of the interest-rate curve, where a decision to issue more longer-dated debt will lead to a steeper curve and a decision to issue more shorter-dated debt will lead to a flatter curve. The increase in the supply of debt in any segment will lower the price of debt in that segment, which leads to higher yields. The overarching principle of Treasury's debt management strategy is to provide the lowest cost of financing to the taxpayer over time. To that end, Treasury will perform its own analysis, along with input from the private sector, to determine the cheapest way to fund the deficit. For example, when the Fed put downward pressure on longer-dated Treasury yields through quantitative easing, the Treasury adjusted its issuance towards longer-dated debt to take advantage of the lower long-term rates.

The Treasury aims to issue debt at a regular and predictable pace, making slight adjustments in size and frequency on a quarterly basis. This is important because of the sheer size of annual issuance, which in recent years is in the trillions of dollars. The market is more easily able to digest the issuance if it can accurately anticipate the amount of debt being issued and prepares accordingly. Surprising the market could lead to yields spiking higher, which would be disruptive. At the beginning of every quarter, the Treasury will announce its estimated financing needs, which is based on expected federal outlays, tax revenues, debt maturities, and the amount of cash on hand it wants to hold at the end of the quarter. The Treasury aims to hold at least enough cash to cover five days of outflows.

When unexpected adjustments in debt issuance must be made, then the Treasury makes up the difference by issuing short-term debt. This is because the market is more able to digest changes in short-term debt than longer-term debt. For example, when Congress passed the $2.2 trillion CARES stimulus package in March 2020, the Treasury met the bulk of the financing need through $1.5 trillion in Treasury bills, which are Treasury securities that mature in less than a year. The bills were easily digested by money market funds, who have over $4 trillion in assets that constantly need to be rolled over into short-term investments. On the other hand, the market for longer-term Treasury securities is populated by investors who have longer time horizons and are less able to react to short-term fluctuations. These investors, which include pension funds, insurance companies, and sovereign funds, will not suddenly have more money to invest if Treasury issuance surges.

The issuing of Treasury securities is different from central bank reserves or bank deposits because it is literally backed by nothing but confidence in the U.S. government. Central bank reserves are backed by the safe assets they purchased, essentially exchanging one type of money for another. Bank deposits are backed by loans, which eventually must be paid back, thus unwinding the amount of money created. The Treasury issues trillions and trillions of dollars' worth of Treasury securities but does not appear to have a plan to repay any of it. Instead, the amount of Treasury securities outstanding continues to grow at an accelerating pace. This has an inflationary impact because goods and services are purchased by printing money, but this is only one factor among many that determine aggregate inflation.

Many market participants have looked at the rising levels of U.S. debt and suggested that a debt crisis is imminent. Yet there are countries like Japan who have a far higher debt-to-GDP ratio than the U.S., and Treasury yields have marched relentlessly lower even as Treasury issuance soared. There is obviously some limit to how much debt the Treasury can issue, but it's not clear what the limit is.

Chapter 3 – The Shadow Banks

The term "shadow bank" sounds mysterious and a bit ominous, but they are just non-commercial-bank businesses that engage in banking-like activity. Like commercial banks, shadow banks take on liquidity and credit risk by creating loans or purchasing assets. However, they cannot create bank deposits the way commercial banks can, so instead, they borrow from investors to fund their assets. Rather than being creators of money, shadow banks are intermediaries.

Shadow banks encompass a wide range of entities that engage in activities that are generally riskier than those of commercial banks. As we discussed in the previous chapter, commercial banks are closely regulated and subject to extensive disclosure requirements. The largest commercial banks even have regulators on-site each day monitoring compliance. But these onerous requirements also come with benefits: commercial banks can borrow from the Fed's discount window and their depositors are protected by FDIC deposit insurance. Shadow banks generally operate under less restrictions than commercial banks. This can lead to higher returns, but their investors do not have the same public sector protections. Instead, investors in shadow banks must rely on alternative private sector protections. These protections include insurance provided by private insurers, hedging derivatives like credit default swaps, or assurances provided by ratings agencies.

The basic business model of a shadow bank is to use shorter-term loans to invest in longer-dated assets. This mismatch creates an opportunity for profit as longer-term interest rates are usually higher than shorter-term interest rates. The shadow bank may also be earning a risk premium by investing in riskier assets. This bank-like business model also makes shadow banks vulnerable to bank runs when their investors refuse to renew their loans. Without access to the Fed as lender of last resort, shadow banks may have to sell assets to meet investor withdrawals. During a panic, they would have to sell assets at large discounts, potentially incurring large losses. The 2008 Financial Crisis and 2020 COVID-19 panic were largely due to runs on the shadow banking system.

The shadow banking system does not adhere to a rigid definition, but usually encompasses entities such as dealers, money market funds, exchange-traded funds (ETFs), investment funds, and securitization vehicles. In recent decades, the shadow banking system has grown to be larger and more influential than the traditional commercial banking system. In the following sections we will introduce a few of the more notable shadow banks: primary dealers, money market funds, exchange-traded funds, mortgage REITs, private investment funds, and securitization vehicles.

Primary Dealers

Primary dealers are a group of dealers that have the privilege of trading directly with the Federal Reserve. They are the heart of the financial system and the primary conduit for Federal Reserve open market operations. The Federal Reserve conducts its monetary operations exclusively through primary dealers.[10] For example, when the Fed is conducting quantitative easing by buying Treasuries, it only buys from primary dealers.[11] There are currently 24 primary dealers, almost all affiliated with large foreign or domestic banks.[12] This is because primary dealers are required to meet certain requirements and obligations that can be very costly for smaller dealers. For example, primary dealers are obligated to make frequent regulatory disclosures,

---

[10] In emergency circumstances, the Fed has also used large asset managers such as PIMCO and Blackrock to manage temporary programs such as the Commercial Paper Funding Facility.

[11] All Treasury trading with the Fed is done through the Fed's proprietary trading software, FedTrade. The Fed puts out an operational schedule telling the primary dealers when they will be operating, and then the primary dealer participates.

[12] For a current list of primary dealers, see https://www.newyorkfed.org/markets/primarydealers.html.

participate in Treasury security auctions, and provide market intelligence to the Desk.

Dealers in general are like supermarkets for financial products. A supermarket buys a whole assortment of goods from producers, stores them, and then sells them at a markup to consumers. In the same way, a dealer stands ready to buy a wide range of financial products like corporate bonds or U.S Treasuries, then holds on to them until it can find other investors willing to buy the products. The dealer will fund its inventory of financial products by borrowing money in the repo market using the financial products as collateral. These are usually overnight loans that the dealer renews every day until they are able to find a buyer for the product. Dealers allow investors to buy and sell securities with ease, without which there could not be a financial system.

In addition to making markets for financial products, dealers also act as financial intermediaries, borrowing from one client to lend to another. For example, a hedge fund may want to take out a one-month loan from a dealer collateralized by some securities. A dealer would make the one-month repo loan, then source the money by borrowing from one of its investor clients using those same securities as collateral. However, the dealer will likely borrow on an overnight basis instead of matching the maturity of the two loans. Since the interest rate for overnight loans is lower than the rate for one-month loans, the dealer will be able to earn the difference between in interest it receives from the one-month loan to the hedge fund and what it pays its investor client for an overnight loan. This type of transaction is called a matched book repo trade, because the two repo transactions offset each other.

Dealers are considered a shadow bank because of the financial intermediation they engage in. The overnight repo loans they borrow are like commercial bank deposits. They take the proceeds from those overnight loans and either lend them to clients or use them to buy securities. This exposes them to risks similar to bank runs where investors may refuse to renew their overnight loans. When that happens, the dealers would be forced to sell securities to repay their overnight loans. As the dealer sells its securities into the market, the selling could put downward pressure on the price of the securities. If this occurs on a large scale, the prices of the securities could decline significantly and spook investors. More investors could refuse to renew their loans, which in turn would lead to more forced selling. Soon, you end up with a financial crisis.

That is exactly what happened in 2008. In March 2008, Bear Stearns, a major investment bank and primary dealer, failed when its investments in the subprime mortgage market soured. When investors heard about Bear Stearns' troubles, they became afraid and refused to renew their repo loans to Bear Stearns. Bear Stearns was thus forced to sell its assets at fire sale prices to repay those loans. This hurt asset prices and led investors to be cautious in their lending to all dealers. It was only when the Fed stepped in as a lender of last resort that confidence was restored and market conditions normalized. The Fed is not usually able to lend to primary dealers, but in this case exercised its emergency lending powers, known as 13(c) after the section in the Federal Reserve Act authorizing them, and established the Primary Dealer Liquidity Facility (PDCF).[13] The PDCF was basically a discount-window facility available only to primary dealers.

How the Fed Bails Out the Shadow Banks

The Fed only transacts with the primary dealers, but, through the primary dealer system, it is able to indirectly reach deeply into the dark corners of the financial system. This is because the primary dealers have relationships with virtually all the major financial institutions in the world. Fed policy is transmitted through these relationships.

The primary dealers provide liquidity for these financial institutions and set the price of that liquidity. When a shadow bank needs money, it calls up a dealer to either sell the financial assets it owns outright for cash or borrow against them. A dealer will quote them a price for the security if they are selling or quote an interest rate if they are borrowing money.

---

[13] "Federal Reserve Announces Two Initiatives Designed to Bolster Market Liquidity and Promote Orderly Market Functioning." Press Release. Board of Governors of the Federal Reserve System, March 16, 2008. https://www.federalreserve.gov/newsevents/pressreleases/monetary20080316a.htm.

While retail investors can logon to their trading account and simply sell their stocks for cash, shadow banks hold many assets that are not exchange traded. For example, corporate bonds and Treasury securities are not exchange traded. Pricing for securities that are not exchange traded are determined by the dealer community, which prices them using computer models and market conditions.

The primary dealers buy securities or offer loans using funds they borrow from other clients, usually money market funds. But they can also borrow from the Fed. The terms of the financing offered by the Fed affect the terms they are willing to offer their shadow bank clients. For example, if primary dealers can borrow from the Fed at 1%, then the interest rates received by the broader market won't be too much higher.

In September 2019, overnight repo rates suddenly spiked from around 2 percent to over 5 percent in a couple days. Remember, dealers are highly dependent on overnight loans because their assets tend to be longer dated securities or loans. The dealer community was having tremendous trouble finding overnight money to borrow and was paying through the nose to entice investors to lend. This panicked the market and prompted the Fed to begin conducting routine repo operations with the primary dealers. In effect, the Fed was willing to lend to primary dealers in unlimited size at below market rates. The primary dealers in turn took that cheap money and further lent it into the market.

During the COVID-19 panic, primary dealers borrowed around $400 billion from the Fed to pay for assets that their shadow bank clients were desperate to sell. Recall that hedge funds, mortgage REITs, and ETFs were all scrambling for cash. In effect, the Fed indirectly bailed them out through the primary dealer system.

The level of primary dealer repo borrowings from the Fed gradually tapered off to zero in the second half of 2020. Massive QE significantly reduced the amount of Treasury and Agency MBS in the financial system, and thus the demand for primary dealer cash.

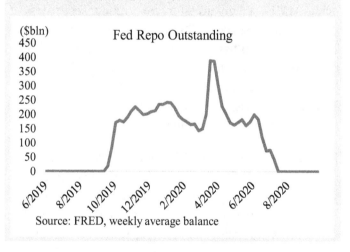

Source: FRED, weekly average balance

Money Market Mutual Funds

A money market fund (MMF) is a special type of investment fund that invests only in short-term securities and allows investors to withdraw their money at any time with next-business-day availability. MMFs are subject to regulations that tightly control the credit quality and tenor of the investments they can make. This makes MMFs a relatively safe investment. Indeed, investors tend to consider MMF investments to be virtually risk-free. One dollar invested in a money fund can almost certainly be withdrawn any business day with no loss. MMF shares are very like bank deposits.

MMFs are broadly divided into two types: government MMFs and prime MMFs. Government MMFs can only invest in government securities, while prime MMFs can also invest in nongovernment securities. In practice, prime MMFs largely invest in government securities and securities issued by foreign commercial banks. Foreign commercial banks are active in corporate banking but generally don't have a retail business. This means they don't have a stable retail deposit base and must instead actively borrow from institutional investors like prime MMFs to manage their outflows.

Investments made by MMFs tend to be very short term, mostly overnight but potentially up to a maximum of 397 days. This is in part due to SEC regulations, which include a number of rules that limit the maturity profile of a MMF's portfolio. The rules are intended to reduce the risk of "bank runs." Because the assets of MMFs mature very quickly, there is always plenty of cash from maturing investments to meet any investor withdrawals. In addition, MMFs tend to have sizable holdings of short-term government securities that can easily be sold to meet outflows.

MMF investments are used by a wide range of investors as bank deposit substitutes. Investors expect to be able to invest $1 in an MMF, earn market interest rates, and withdraw that $1 when needed. However, MMFs are not commercial banks, so they do not have access to the Fed's discount window and their investors are not protected by deposit insurance. This lack of government backstop could leave their investors vulnerable in times of panic, at least in the case of prime MMFs. In practice, institutional investors are actually more comfortable leaving large amounts of money with prime MMFs than with commercial banks. This is because prime MMFs diversify their exposure by investing in many banks, while leaving large amounts of money at a single commercial bank concentrates risk.

MMFs are a key source of cash for the shadow banking world. This is because money invested in an MMF is moved around the financial system through intermediation chains that can be long. For example, an investor can invest in an MMF, which then lends to a dealer through a repo loan, who in turn lends to a hedge fund through a matched book repo.

When the Money Market Funds Crashed

Investors view MMFs investments like bank deposits—every $1 invested in an MMF can be withdrawn without loss, just like deposits in a commercial bank checking account. That assumption failed in September 2008 when one of the largest MMFs, the Reserve Primary Fund, incurred losses on loans it made to failed investment bank Lehman Brothers.[14] Those losses meant that $1 of investment in the Reserve Primary Fund was worth less than $1.

When investors began to see that they had lost money in their money market investments, they panicked and withdrew their money en masse. Within a few days, investors had withdrawn $42 billion from the fund, which had held $65 billion earlier in the month.[15] This forced the Reserve Primary Fund to sell assets in fire sale conditions to meet investor withdrawals, which led to more investor losses. Investors then looked around at other prime MMFs and began to be afraid that other funds might also "break the buck."

This led to a run on all prime MMFs, which were major lenders to commercial banks. Now that commercial banks were losing prime MMF funding, they were forced raise the interest rates in an attempt to attract new investors. When the market saw the short-term interest rates these commercial banks were offering, they began to suspect that some banks may be insolvent. This in turn led to even more panic throughout the financial system.

---

[14] Baba, Naohiko, Robert McCauley, and Srichander Ramaswamy. "US Dollar Money Market Funds and Non-US Banks." *BIS Quarterly Review*, March 2009, 65–81. https://www.bis.org/publ/qtrpdf/r_qt0903g.pdf.
[15] "Reserve Primary Fund Drops below $1 a Share amid Lehman Fall." *Reuters*, September 16, 2008. https://www.reuters.com/article/us-reservefund-buck-idUSN1669401520080916.

During this emergency, the Fed and the Treasury stepped in to calm markets. The Treasury announced a Temporary Guarantee Program for Money Market Funds, which essentially protected MMF investors from loss, similar to FDIC bank deposit insurance. The Fed announced the Money Market Investor Funding Facility, which would stand ready to buy assets from MMFs in case they needed to sell assets to meet investor withdrawals. The MMF complex stabilized following these announcements of government support.

Exchange Traded Funds

ETFs are investment funds whose shares are traded on an exchange like a stock. An ETF takes an investor's money and uses it to purchase assets such as stocks, bonds, or commodity futures. For example, a Treasury ETF would issue shares and use the proceeds to buy Treasury securities. An S&P 500 Index ETF would issue shares and use the proceeds to buy the stocks underlying the S&P 500 Index. A key benefit of ETFs is their liquidity. Because ETF shares are traded on an exchange, an investor can sell their shares any time the market is open.

In theory, the price of a share of an ETF should reflect the value of the ETF's assets. An ETF with 100 shares outstanding that holds $1000 worth of a basket of stocks should have a stock price of $10. The relationship between the price on an ETF share and its underlying asset value is policed by institutional investors who make money by arbitraging the ETF's share price and underlying fund asset values. Following the example, if the share price of the ETF were $9, then an institutional investor could purchase one share and then request the ETF to redeem that share for 1% of its assets, which is $10 worth of stock. The institutional investor can then sell that $10 worth of stock on the market and realize a profit of $1. If the share price of the ETF were instead $11, then the investor could purchase a basket of stocks that mimic the composition of the ETF's assets and then ask the ETF to buy the stock in exchange for 1 share. The institutional investor can then sell that share on the market for a profit of $1.

An ETF is shadow bank because, while its shares can be sold any time the market is open, the assets the ETF holds may not be as liquid. This is especially true for corporate bond ETFs or ETFs that hold small cap stocks. Corporate bonds and small cap stocks do not trade very frequently, so any sudden wave of selling would lead to very large price moves. In principle, the redemption structure for ETFs make them less vulnerable to runs because a redemption of an ETF share yields a basket of securities, so the ETF itself is not subject to forced selling of its underlying assets. However, should an institutional investor try to arbitrage the difference by redeeming its shares for securities and then selling the underlying securities, then that could lead to a cycle of larger downward price moves that could lead to more redemptions.

In the 2020 COVID-19 panic, investors sold ETF shares so aggressively that many ETFs were trading significantly below fund asset values. Institutional investors were having trouble arbitraging the differences because market conditions were so poor that even if they could redeem their ETF shares for the underlying securities, they could not sell them: there were no buyers for the securities.

Mortgage REITs

Mortgage REITs (mREITs) are investment funds that invest in mortgage-backed securities, usually Agency MBS securities guaranteed by Fannie Mae or Freddie Mac. They are classic shadow banks that take out very short-term loans to invest in very long-term assets. The typical mREIT will buy mortgage securities that mature in 15 to 30 years using one-month repo loans that are continually renewed.

Even with long-term Treasury security yields at historical lows, mREITs have been able to provide annual interest in excess of 10%. They are particularly popular with retail investors who are looking for interest income. mREITs are able to provide those yields through leverage that can be as high as 8x their capital. For example, an mREIT could borrow in the repo market at 0.3% at a one-month tenor and then invest in a 30-year mortgage security yielding 2.5% to earn a net interest margin of 2.2%. With just 5x leverage that would yield annual interest income of over 10%. To the extent that the mortgage securities are guaranteed, then mREITs do not take on any credit risk. However, they are very vulnerable to bank-run-like shocks where they are unable to renew their repo loans. Such a shock occurred during the 2020 COVID-19 panic.

During the 2020 COVID-19 panic, there were significant dislocations across markets, including the usually very liquid Agency MBS market. Dealers who had provided repo loans to the mREITs against Agency MBS collateral became less sure about the value of the collateral and began demanding that the mREITs put up more cash as collateral. At the same time, many mREITs had experienced losses from their interest-rate hedges and were short on cash. To meet these demands for cash, the mREITs were forced to sell their Agency RMBS securities at a time when there was very little liquidity in the market. The fire sale forced prices lower, which in turn led to more fire sales and forced many mREITs to realize heavy losses. Over the course of a few weeks, mREIT investors lost over half of their investment and, in some cases, more.

iShares Mortgage ETF Share Price

Source: Bloomberg

Private Investment Funds

Private investment funds, such as hedge funds or private equity funds, take investor money and invest in a broad spectrum of financial assets. These funds employ a very wide range of strategies, so it is difficult to generalize. Some invest in illiquid assets that could include equity of non–publicly traded companies, U.S. dollar–denominated foreign debt, and farmland across the world. Others invest in liquid securities such as publicly traded stocks. Investors in private funds usually cannot withdraw their money on demand but have agreed to keep it invested in the fund for a certain period of time. In a sense, private investment funds borrow medium term and invest long term. This set up allows the funds to avoid fire sales of their assets to meet investor withdrawals. However, some private investment funds do employ more aggressive strategies that rely on short-term borrowing. This behavior would make them vulnerable to bank run like risks should their lenders decide to not renew their loans.

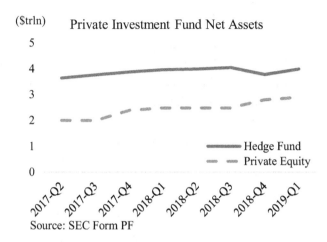

($trln) Private Investment Fund Net Assets

Source: SEC Form PF

Cash-Futures Basis Blow-up

The Treasury market cash-futures basis trade is one where investors earn money by arbitraging the difference between pricing on a Treasury futures contract and pricing on a Treasury security in the cash market. A Treasury futures contract is an agreement to deliver a Treasury security at a predetermined price at a specific date in the future. When the Treasury futures prices are higher than the Treasury cash market, an investor can potentially profit by selling the Treasury futures, buying Treasuries in the cash market, and then delivering the purchased cash Treasuries to satisfy the futures contract at expiration. The investor would pocket the difference between the futures price and cash price.

Investors usually put this trade on by financing their cash Treasury position in the repo market. The trade would be profitable if the pricing difference between the futures prices and cash prices (the cash-futures basis) was wide enough to compensate for the financing costs of the repo loan. The basis is generally very narrow, so investors must employ a very large amount of leverage to generate meaningful profits. The trade theoretically locks in a profit at inception, but there is always the possibility that the basis widens further before converging at settlement. To the extent that the repo loans were very short term, an investor would also bear the risk of repo interest rates rising and thus narrowing or eliminating the potential profit. Overall, the Treasury cash-futures basis trade is considered a low-risk trade as both Treasury futures and Treasury securities move in the same direction and are very liquid, so an investor could unwind the trade quickly if things went poorly.

During the COVID-19 panic, the Treasury cash-futures basis trade went spectacularly wrong.[16] During the crisis, interest rates declined as the Fed lowered its target rate to the zero lower bound and investors purchased Treasuries in a flight to safety. However, the Treasury futures market moved much more than the Treasury cash market. The Treasury cash market essentially broke as dealers were no longer able to make markets. This caused the cash-futures basis to widen significantly and investors to take heavy losses on their futures positions. Those losses were magnified by leverage, which could even reach 100x. The relative value hedge funds that put on the trade were forced to

---

[16] Schrimpf, Andreas, Hyun Song Shin, and Vladyslav Sushko. "Leverage and Margin Spirals in Fixed Income Markets during the Covid-19 Crisis." BIS Bulletin No 2. BIS, April 2, 2020. https://www.bis.org/publ/bisbull02.htm.

unwind it by selling their Treasury securities at a time when there was little market liquidity, further pushing prices down and increasing their losses. Many hedge funds took enormous losses on these trades.[17]

Securitization

Securitization is a financing structure where a pool of il-liquid financial assets is funded by issuing bonds to investors. Generally speaking, a commercial bank originates a loan and then sells it to a securitization vehicle, who buys the loan using the proceeds of bonds it issues. The securitization vehicles can buy hundreds or thousands of loans and issue different bonds, each with distinct risk profiles. The principal and interest payments from the loans are used to pay off the bond investors. Different risk profiles are created for each bond according to the priority in which bonds are paid off, where bonds that are highest in the payment waterfall are considered the lowest risk. The owners of the securitization vehicle receive any leftover payments after all the bond investors are paid off. A securitization vehicle is like a bank in that it is borrowing from investors to take on credit and liquidity risk.

---

[17] Basak, Sonali, Liz McCormick, Donal Griffin, and Hema Parmar. "Before Fed Acted, Leverage Burned Hedge Funds in Treasury Market." *Bloomberg*, March 19, 2020. https://www.bloomberg.com/news/articles/2020-03-19/before-fed-acted-leverage-burned-hedge-funds-in-treasury-trade.

The most well-known type of securitized asset are mortgage loans, but auto loans, credit card loans, and student loans are also common. Virtually any financial asset that provides a stable cash flow can be securitized, including assets like fast food chain franchise fees, cell phone payments or music royalties. Securitization provides investors an opportunity to invest in a wide range of asset classes and allows borrowers to tap a wider range of investors.

The rise of securitization played an important role in the 2008 Financial Crisis by fundamentally changing the business model of many commercial banks. Traditionally, a commercial bank held on to the loans it originated, so it was careful who it lent to. A commercial bank could easily end up bankrupt if just 5% of its loan assets were written off. But the rise of securitization meant a commercial bank could earn fees by originating a loan and selling it to a securitization vehicle. Many commercial banks began to transition their business model from earning interest on loans to earning fees on originating loans. Since they did not hold the loans themselves, commercial banks were less interested if a loan soured. That was a risk borne by the securitization bond investors.

When Shadow Banks Emerge from the Shadows

In August 2007, there was a run in a relatively obscure part of the shadow banking sector—the Asset-Backed

Commercial Paper (ABCP) market.[18] ABCPs are investment vehicles that borrow short term in the money markets by issuing commercial paper (which is unsecured debt that usually matures within a few months) and then investing the proceeds in longer tenor and more illiquid financial assets. These assets vary according to the ABCP, but could be bank loans, corporate receivables, or securities. The ABCP continually issues and rolls over short-term debt to finance its assets. At a high level, ABCPs are like commercial banks but funded by short-term money market debt.

However, investors in ABCP did not benefit from the public protections offered to commercial banks so turned to private sector sources of protection. ABCP investors did not have the benefit of stringent banking regulations protecting their investment, so they relied on the judgement of ratings agencies to determine how safe their investments were. ABCP investors also did not benefit from the safety of FDIC deposit insurance, so instead relied on guarantees from an ABCP's sponsor. The ABCP's sponsor, which is usually a commercial bank, manages the ABCP and usually stands ready to buy back any ABCP commercial paper if the ABCP's assets sour.

---

[18] For more on the topic, see Covitz, Daniel M., J. Nellie Liang, and Gustavo A. Suarez. "The Anatomy of a Financial Crisis: The Evolution of Panic-Driven Runs in the Asset-Backed Commercial Paper Market." *Proceedings, Federal Reserve Bank of San Francisco*, January 2009, 1–36.

In July 2007, a couple large hedge funds with sizable investments in subprime-mortgage-related assets were liquidated, and in the first week of August, American Home Mortgage, a large subprime lender, filed for bankruptcy. That meant an ABCP vehicle that American Home Mortgage sponsored would lose its guarantees at a time when the market was losing confidence in the value of subprime-mortgage-related assets. Market participants began to worry about the asset quality of the entire ABCP sector and refused to renew their loans. In July of 2007, ABCPs had $1.163 trillion assets outstanding, but a month later, that had declined almost $200 billion to $0.976 trillion.

The panic in the ABCP sector spilled over into the commercial banking sector through the guarantees made by commercial bank sponsors. As ABCP investors refused to renew their debt, commercial banks were forced to step in and finance the assets held by the ABCPs. This put strains on the liquidity of commercial banks and also potentially subjected them to credit losses. Interbank interest rates shot up in reflection of these concerns, forcing both the Fed and the ECB to step in to calm markets. Both American and European commercial banks were active as ABCP sponsors, so the issue crossed national boundaries.

The ABCP market stabilized as central bank actions calmed investors, but little did investors know that this was only the first tremors of what would, one year later, be an existential event for the financial system. The next warning came with the collapse of Bear Stearns a few months later in early 2008, which was discussed in an earlier section.

Federal Home Loan Banks: The Government-Backed Shadow Bank

Government-sponsored enterprises (GSEs) play a large, important, but often unnoticed role in the financial markets and the real economy. GSEs are entities that are technically not part of the federal government but are assumed to be implicitly guaranteed by it. Unlike private corporations, GSEs are not profit driven but seek to further public policy goals such as supporting residential housing. The most well-known GSEs are Fannie and Freddie, but the largest is actually the Federal Home Loan Bank (FHLB) system.

The FHLB system was first established in 1932 to support the housing sector by providing loans to commercial banks. It currently comprises 11 regional FHLBs who are each organized as cooperatives. Each FHLB is owned by its member commercial banks, who must purchase stock in the FHLB to become members. These commercial banks share in any losses of the FHLB and receive its profits through dividend payments. Foreign banks are ineligible for FHLB membership.

FHLBs borrow from institutional investors and then lend to their member banks. They are essentially government-backed shadow banks that aim to support commercial banks. In practice, FHLBs largely borrow on a short-term basis from government MMFs and lend to member banks at slightly longer tenors. Because they are implicitly guaranteed by the government, FHLBs are able to borrow at very low interest rates and pass those low rates along to their members. These rates are generally lower than what a member commercial bank can borrow at in the market, especially if it is a bank with a low credit rating.

FHLBs will lend to a commercial bank as long as it provides adequate collateral. This makes FHLB loans an important source of financing when market conditions are poor and private sector financing becomes scarce. When under stress, commercial banks will first borrow from the FHLBs and only go to the Fed's discount window as a last resort because of the stigma attached to discount-window borrowing. With around $1 trillion in assets, the FHLB system has a sizable footprint in the financial system.

Historically, small- and medium-sized banks were the primary borrowers from the FHLBs. These banks had limited access to wholesale funding, so FHLB loans were the easiest way for them to get cheap loans. In recent years, the largest borrowers from FHLBs have been the biggest U.S. banks.[19] This is because big banks are subject to stricter Basel III regulations that push

---

[19] Gissler, Stefan, and Borghan Narajabad. "The Increased Role of the Federal Home Loan Bank System in Funding Markets." FEDS Notes. Board of Governors of the Federal Reserve System, October 18, 2017. https://doi.org/10.17016/2380-7172.2070.

them to have stable liabilities. Under Basel III, FHLB loans are considered stable because FHLBs are government-sponsored enterprises.

Chapter 4 – The Eurodollar Market

Eurodollars are U.S. dollars held outside of the United States. They are called Eurodollars because the first off-shore dollars appeared in Europe in 1956.[20] The Euro-dollar market grew in part as a regulatory arbitrage by commercial banks, but also in response to growing demand by foreigners for dollars. The Bretton Woods Agreement in 1944 had created a new monetary system that shifted the world from a gold standard to a U.S. dollar standard. Widespread use of the dollar grew in tandem with the U.S.' ascension to a global hegemon and persisted even as the relative dominance of the U.S. declined with the establishment of the European Union and rise of China. The global dollar system extends the

---

[20] Murau, Steffen, Joe Rini, and Armin Haas. "The Evolution of the Offshore US-Dollar System: Past, Present and Four Possible Futures." *Journal of Institutional Economics*, 2020, 1–17.
https://doi.org/10.1017/S1744137420000168. See also He, Dong, and Robert N. McCauley. "Eurodollar Banking and Currency Internationalisation." *BIS Quarterly Review*, June 2012, 33–46.
https://www.bis.org/publ/qtrpdf/r_qt1206f.htm.

influence, and perhaps the responsibility, of the Fed far beyond the borders of the U.S.

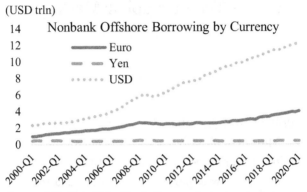

Source: BIS Global Liquidty Indicators, Author's calculations

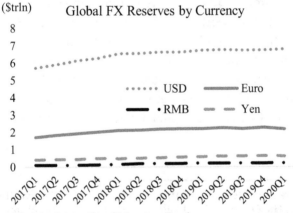

Source: International Monetary Fund

There are offshore markets for euros, yen, and other currencies, but none of them come close to the size of the offshore U.S. dollar market. The amount of dollar borrowing by nonbanks residing outside the U.S. is around $13 trillion, far surpassing the offshore demand for other major currencies such as the euro and yen. Looking at official foreign exchange holdings, the U.S. dollar is the clear favorite with around 60% of all foreign reserves being held in dollars. There is a clear global demand for dollars that does not exist for any other currency. That demand can be attributed to a few factors.

Safety. The U.S. dollar is widely considered to be a global safe haven. Whenever there is distress in the world, investors rush into the U.S. dollar. The U.S. dollar is backed by the world's strongest military, largest economy, a relatively impartial legal system, and a central bank that has kept inflation stable for decades. U.S.-based investors may take all this for granted, but these benefits are not widely seen elsewhere in the world. Many countries struggle with high inflation due to poor government management or suffer bouts of existential risk. For example, Argentina has endured annual inflation rates over the past years that ranged from 10 to 50%. Consequently, many Argentinians prefer to hold their savings in dollars. In 2011, the Euro depreciated significantly against the dollar as concerns emerged that the European Union may dissolve. Concerns for the future of the European Union have ebbed and flowed as the U.K. left and anti-EU political parties gained in popularity in some EU countries.

Trade. Global trade essentially operates on a dollar standard, where around 50% of global trade is invoiced in dollars and around 40% of international payments are made in dollars.[21] The dollar is used in trade even when none of the parties are American. For example, when Japan imports oil from Saudi Arabia, they pay in dollars. When a Korean electronics manufacturer buys components from a Thai contractor, the payment is likely to be in dollars. There is a very strong "network effect" for U.S. dollars, much like paying with Mastercard or Visa. Everyone accepts dollars, so everyone holds them.

In addition to international acceptance, a large portion of the world also has limited exchange rate risk when holdings dollars. This is because much of the world economy uses currencies that closely track the dollar, which makes holding dollars a substitute for holding the local currency. From this perspective, the dollar essentially forms a "currency bloc" that accounts for over 50% of global GDP.[22] The bloc includes countries like Saudi Arabia, which explicitly pegs its currency to the dollar, as well as large countries like China and Mexico, who both previously pegged their currencies to the dollar.

---

[21] BIS Working Group. "US Dollar Funding: An International Perspective." CGFS Papers No. 65. BIS Committee on the Global Financial System, June 2020. https://www.bis.org/publ/cgfs65.htm.

[22] McCauley, Robert N., and Hiro Ito. "A Key Currency View of Global Imbalances." BIS Working Papers No. 762. BIS, December 2018. https://www.bis.org/publ/work762.htm.

Lower cost. Foreigners sometimes prefer borrowing in dollars when the interest rates on dollar loans or bonds are lower than those in their home currency.[23] When the Federal Reserve sets short-term interest rates in the U.S. at a level that is low relative to other countries, then interest rates of bank loans in dollars also become relatively low and attractive to foreign borrowers. This is especially true in emerging markets like China or Brazil, where interest rates on local currency bank loans can be a few percentage points higher than loans in dollars. In a similar way, when the Fed conducts quantitative easing to lower yields on U.S. Treasury securities, then the borrowing rate for private sector dollar bonds, which are priced based on Treasury yields, also decline. A foreign borrower may find that the interest rate they pay for borrowing in dollars is lower than borrowing in their home currency and decide to borrow in dollars.

Liquidity. Dollar capital markets are the deepest and most liquid in the world. Many foreign countries do not have capital markets that are as sophisticated as the dollar capital markets, so they choose instead to borrow in dollars. For example, Australian banks find it easier to borrow in U.S. dollars even when they want to invest in Australian dollar assets. The size of the U.S. dollar capital markets allows them to access a wide range of investors and more easily borrow large sums than they could in Australian markets. The Australian banks

---

[23] McCauley, Robert N., Patrick McGuire, and Vladyslav Sushko. "Global Dollar Credit: Links to US Monetary Policy and Leverage." BIS Working Papers No. 483. BIS, January 2015. https://www.bis.org/publ/work483.htm.

would then exchange the U.S. dollars for Australian dollars in a swap transaction. In other instances, the ease of issuing dollar debt complements the dollar's dominant role in global trade. A foreign corporation holds dollars both because it needs it to make payments and because issuing dollar-denominated debt is the easiest for them.

In the same way, holding dollars can be desirable because they are easy to store. A deep and liquid Treasury market means investors can easily store even large quantities of dollars risk-free. Recall, Treasuries are just money that pays interest. Liquidity is a real concern for institutions or wealthy individuals who have a lot of money. A big part of the reason China owns trillions in Treasuries even though they are not very friendly with the U.S. is because they have no alternative; there is no other market deep enough to hold all that money.

The discussion above shows why foreigners would want to hold dollars, but it doesn't explain why those dollars are held offshore. There are a few reasons why foreigners hold their dollars offshore.[24] Just as Americans have a natural bias to hold dollars in the U.S., foreigners have a natural bias to hold dollars in their home country. This could be because they are more familiar with banks in their home country, it could be more

---

[24] He, Dong, and Robert N. McCauley. "Offshore Markets for the Domestic Currency: Monetary and Financial Stability Issues." BIS Working Papers No. 320. BIS, September 2010. https://www.bis.org/publ/work320.htm.

convenient for them to hold dollars locally, or it could be they distrust the U.S. government. For example, the Soviet Union deposited its dollars in London. Holding dollars offshore is a way for investors to separate currency risk from country risk. Finally, offshore banks have historically offered higher interest rates on their deposits than banks in the U.S.

The offshore dollar market comprises offshore dollar banking and offshore dollar capital markets. Both are sizable at around $6.5 trillion each when taking into account only lending to nonbank borrowers. The bulk of the lending in the offshore dollar market does not come from U.S. sources but from other offshore sources. U.S. resident banks are relatively minor lenders with around $1.6 trillion in bank credit to offshore nonbank borrowers. Data from the U.S. Treasury estimates U.S.-based investment funds hold $2.6 trillion of debt issued by the offshore borrowers, though that also includes securities issued by bank borrowers.

Banks and investors are willing to lend to offshore borrowers because it offers them a way to diversify their portfolio and an opportunity to earn higher returns. Offshore borrowers usually have a more limited source of dollars, so they are willing to pay higher interest rates for dollars than a U.S.-resident borrower. Also, many offshore borrowers are located in emerging markets with higher economic growth rates that allow them to afford higher interest rates. Investing offshore also allows banks and investors an opportunity to diversify their portfolio holdings across countries and thus reduce political risk.

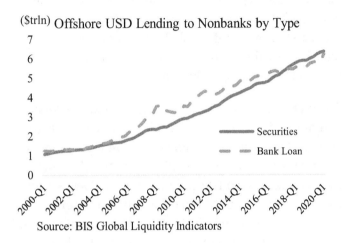

(\$trln) Offshore USD Lending to Nonbanks by Type

Source: BIS Global Liquidity Indicators

Offshore Dollar Banking

The offshore dollar banking system can be divided into two segments: one that exists primarily due to regulatory arbitrage and one that is centered on the dollar banking needs of foreigners. Overall, the size of the offshore banking system is around \$10 trillion as of 2018,[25] accounting for roughly a third of the size of the global dollar banking system.[26] Note that this is larger

---

[25] Aldasoro, Iñaki, and Torsten Ehlers. "The Geography of Dollar Funding of Non-US Banks." *BIS Quarterly Review*, December 2018, 15–26. https://www.bis.org/publ/qtrpdf/r_qt1812b.htm.

[26] Onshore deposit taking institutions have around \$20 trillion in dollar liabilities, based on the Federal Reserve's

than the $6.5 trillion in offshore dollar bank loans described above because banks will also hold dollar assets other than loans, such as Treasuries or other debt securities.

The regulatory-arbitrage segment of the offshore banking system has ebbed and flowed over the past few decades. In the first phase, U.S. banks discovered that they could evade onshore banking regulations by moving their banking activity to offshore banking centers like the Cayman Islands or London. Offshore dollar deposits were first seen in London in the 1950s but grew significantly in the 1970s. U.S. banks at the time were bound by Regulation Q and Regulation D. Under Regulation Q, U.S. banks were subject to a ceiling on the level of interest they could pay on their domestic deposits. Under Regulation D, U.S. banks had to hold a certain amount of central bank reserves against their deposit liabilities. However, deposits booked outside the U.S. fell outside of the purview of those regulations. U.S. banks thus had an incentive to grow their business offshore where they could offer high interest rates to attract investors and expand their loan books without worrying about their reserve ratios. In practice, they would simply have their domestic clients make deposits in their offshore branch office, and then have the

----

H8 and the NCUA's quarterly reports on credit unions. Foreign bank dollar liabilities booked outside of the U.S. are around $10 trillion, based on BIS data. FDIC reports show domestic banks have a $1.4 trillion in deposits in their offshore branches, but its not clear how much of the deposits are denominated in dollars.

branch office send the money back onshore to the head office. While the banking transaction was technically offshore and international, it was functionally conducted purely within the U.S. banking system. These flows persisted even as changes to regulation did away with the regulatory advantages of offshore banking. However, after the financial crisis, U.S. banks significantly scaled back their offshore banking as they retrenched and were more mindful of risk management.

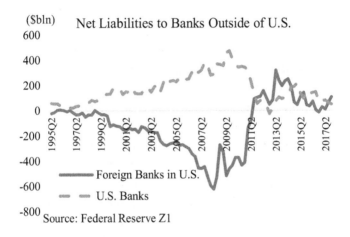

($bln)   Net Liabilities to Banks Outside of U.S.

Source: Federal Reserve Z1

The second wave of regulatory-driven offshore banking came from the European banks in the years leading up to the financial crisis. At the time, the European banks were subject to more lenient regulatory metrics that allowed them to conduct risky trades in much larger sizes than U.S. banks could.[27] The European banks were very

---

[27] He, Dong, and Robert N. McCauley. "Eurodollar Banking and Currency Internationalisation." *BIS Quarterly*

interested in investing in U.S. mortgage-related assets and put on large positions that were largely funded in the U.S. money markets. For example, a U.S. office of a European bank would borrow from U.S. money market funds and send the money back to its European head office, which would then invest the proceeds back into U.S. mortgage assets. European banks were essentially borrowing from onshore U.S. investors and then sending the money back onshore to invest in U.S. assets. These flows largely unwound after the financial crisis as European banks took significant losses from their investments.

The regulatory-driven flows of the offshore banking system were large, but they were basically different ways of intermediating U.S. banking flows. Money from U.S.-resident depositors were ultimately used to fund U.S.-based assets. These flows declined significantly after the financial crisis as both European and U.S. banks retrenched. In recent years, most of the offshore dollar banking flows do not involve the U.S. at all, but are between two foreign entities.[28] An example would be a Japanese bank offering a dollar loan to a Korean company.

These pure offshore flows have always been a significant part of offshore banking activity, but are now more dominant as regulatory-driven flows declined. The pure offshore dollar banking model is comparable to

---

Review, June 2012, 33–46.
https://www.bis.org/publ/qtrpdf/r_qt1206f.htm.
[28] Ibid.

domestic banking, just that it occurs outside of the U.S. Foreigners want dollars, and so the offshore banking system creates dollars for them to hold.[29] The offshore banks active in making dollar loans are the same big global foreign banks we often see in the U.S. U.S. banks in comparison, are less active in making loans to offshore borrowers.

One very important difference between the offshore dollar banking world and the domestic world is with the clients that they primarily serve. The offshore dollar banking world primarily serves corporations and institutional investors, while the domestic banking sector primarily serves retail clients. Foreign retail clients transact primarily in their home country's currency, so they have limited dollar needs. This difference in clientele has significant implications on the funding profile of the offshore banks that operate a dollar business.

While domestic banks can rely on stable retail deposits, offshore banks must manage their funding via money markets using instruments such as institutional certificates of deposit (CDs) and foreign exchange (FX) swaps. This means offshore dollar banking is more susceptible to bank runs. In times of financial market turmoil, retail depositors tend to stay put because their deposits are guaranteed by the government. But institutional investors have investments far in excess of any

---

[29] Friedman, Milton. "The Euro-Dollar Market: Some First Principles." *Federal Reserve Bank of St. Louis Review* 53 (July 1971): 6–24. https://doi.org/10.20955/r.53.16-24.xqk.

government insurance limits, so they are very sensitive to financial market conditions and will quickly move their money out of commercial banks and into risk-free assets at the first sign of trouble. This means that in times of turmoil, institutional investors will not roll over their CD and FX-swap lending, leaving dependent banks scrambling for funding at any cost. During the COVID-19 panic, foreign banks borrowed almost $500 billion in emergency Fed FX-swap loans to meet their funding needs.

How Does a Foreign Bank Create Dollars?

In our prior examples, we showed how U.S. banks create dollars as they create loans but settle interbank payments using central bank reserves. If a foreign bank has an account at the Fed, then it would operate in the same way. Big foreign banks generally have Fed accounts, but smaller ones may not. A smaller foreign bank can build a dollar loan business as well, but it will instead use dollar deposits at a U.S. bank to settle interbank payments. In effect, the smaller foreign bank is creating a fractional banking system built upon a fractional banking system.

For example, suppose a small foreign bank creates a $100 loan to a foreign company. On its balance sheet the small foreign bank holds $50 in deposits at BUSA, a big U.S. bank, as its reserves, and owes the foreign business $100 in dollars in deposits from the loan. Suppose the foreign business makes a $10 payment to its supplier, who banks with CUSA, a U.S. bank. Then the small foreign bank must settle a payment of $10 with

CUSA. The small foreign bank will ask BUSA to make a payment to CUSA on its behalf. BUSA makes the payment by taking $10 in its central bank reserves and paying it to the reserve account of CUSA. BUSA then deducts $10 from the $50 in deposits it owes the small foreign bank.

Foreign company (FCo) borrows $100 from Small European Bank (SEB) and buys $10 of supplies

Assets	Liabilities
+ $100 Deposits at SEB - $10 to pay S +$10 supplies from S	+$100 Loan

SEB sends $10 payment to S

Assets	Liabilities
$50 Deposit at BUSA + $100 Loan to FCo -$10 Deposit at BUSA	Equity +$100 Deposit to FCo -$10 Deposit sent to S

Supplier (S) receives payment from FCo

Assets	Liabilities
+ $10 Deposits at CUSA - $10 Supplies sold	

Supplier's Bank (CUSA) receives payment from BUSA

Assets	Liabilities
Loans +$10 Reserves from BUSA	Equity +$10 Deposit to S

Big U.S. Bank (BUSA) makes payment for SEB

Assets	Liabilities
Loans -$10 Reserves to CUSA	Equity -$10 Deposit to SEB

This illustration shows a couple of important things. First, central bank reserve ratios together with the quantity of central bank reserves do not limit the size of the banking sector. The Eurodollar system can use bank deposits as if they were central bank reserves, and thus expand virtually without limit. Suppose there was $100 in reserves and a reserve ratio of 10, then that implies that total domestic deposits cannot exceed $1000. But if a foreign bank held $100 in those deposits, it could use them as reserves to also make dollar loans and create dollar deposits. The foreign bank wouldn't be under Federal Reserve regulation, so they would be free to decide their own reserve ratio, which could be higher or lower depending on their risk tolerance. Remember, the lower reserves a bank holds the more profitable it would be, but also the likely it would experience trouble meeting withdrawals and possibly collapse under a bank run.

The second point is that the growth of money is driven by bank profitability. If there are many quality borrowers willing to borrow at profitable rates, then a bank will make the loans. The profitability of a bank's loan is largely dependent on its net interest margin, which is the difference between the interest it earns on the loan and its funding costs. Ideally, it will have many retail deposits at 0% interest, but if not, it will have to go to the money markets and borrow funds at market rates. One way to estimate the general profitability of the commercial banking is to look at the steepness of the yield curve, specifically the spread between 3-month bills and the 10-year Treasury. A wider spread suggests a more profitable banking sector, which in turn is positive for economic growth.

Not All Deposits Are the Same

The 2008 Financial Crisis was centered on the banking sector. Banks (and shadow banks) held bad assets and thus could potentially have been insolvent, so many depositors panicked and withdrew their deposits. Banks sold assets to meet withdrawals, which led asset prices to fall, fueling more panic. In response to that episode, the global regulators devised a new set of regulations called Basel III that were designed to make banks safer, but they also changed the structure of dollar banking.

Basel III made banks safer by forcing banks to hold more high-quality liquid assets like Treasury securities and also encouraged them to have more reliable liabilities.[30] The regulators classified bank liabilities according to how "flighty" the liability would be in a time of stress, with retail deposits being the stickiest and unsecured deposits from banks or shadow banks the most unreliable. Retail depositors benefit from FDIC insurance and have little reason to panic, while banks and shadow banks often have to withdraw their deposits in order to meet their own investors' withdrawals.

The change in regulatory treatment forced many banks to fundamentally restructure their liabilities. Large domestic banks were subject to the heaviest regulatory

---

[30] This regulation is called the Liquidity Coverage Ratio.

burden, so they pushed out many of their shadow bank clients and attempted to increase their footprint in retail banking. The shadow banks in turn began to move their money to medium-sized U.S. banks or foreign banks, both of whom were under less stringent versions of Basel III regulation.

This structural shift was further enhanced by reforms in the Dodd-Frank Act that led to a change in the way FDIC insurance fees were calculated.[31] FDIC fees are assessed on U.S. banks to fund the FDIC insurance that banks offer their depositors. Previously, the FDIC assessed fees based on the amount of domestic deposits a U.S. bank held. The new assessment regime significantly broadened the assessment base to all assets minus tangible equity and made risk-based adjustments. The effect of these changes was to encourage U.S. banks to reduce their borrowings from institutional investors in money markets, and instead rely on stabler retail deposits. The U.S. banks followed that incentive and reduced their borrowing in the money markets. The institutional investors instead redeposited their money into foreign banks, which are not FDIC insured and thus not subject to FDIC assessment fees.

---

[31] Kreicher, Lawrence L., Robert N. McCauley, and Patrick McGuire. "The 2011 FDIC Assessment on Banks Managed Liabilities: Interest Rate and Balance-Sheet Responses." BIS Working Papers No. 413. BIS, May 2013. https://www.bis.org/publ/work413.htm.

In effect, regulation shifted large amounts of institutional money out of domestic banks and into foreign banks, sometimes into their offshore offices.

Offshore U.S. Dollar Capital Markets

Borrowers can also obtain dollars by issuing dollar-denominated bonds outside of the United States. In recent years, the outstanding amount of offshore dollar bonds has grown at a faster rate than that of offshore dollar bank loans. A wide range of borrowers issue dollar securities offshore, including foreign governments, foreign corporations, foreign banks, and even U.S. companies.

Borrowers who issue offshore dollar bonds usually have a choice of either borrowing from a bank or issuing a bond, and decide to issue bonds because it is cheaper. Interest rates on bonds are usually benchmarked off U.S Treasury yields, which have remained historically low since the 2008 Financial Crisis. The dynamics behind the growth in offshore dollar bond issuance is similar to what is seen onshore, where low interest rates have led to a flood of corporate bond issuance.

Offshore dollar bonds can be issued from any jurisdiction but are commonly issued in major financial centers like London. Major financial centers are home to bankers with deep expertise in capital markets and to large investment funds who may be interested in purchasing the bonds. In practice, the offshore dollar bonds tend be issued under English law or New York law, since those legal systems are held in higher regard by the international community. In the event of a dispute, investors could take the borrower to court in New York or London, obtain a judgement, and then seek to enforce that judgement. The enforcement aspect can be tricky, since the borrower's assets may be located in a jurisdiction that does not acknowledge the judgement. Investors in defaulted Argentinian government dollar-denominated bonds famously took a default judgement by U.S. courts and used it to seize Argentinian ships docked at foreign ports as payment.[32]

Investors in offshore dollar bonds include both U.S. resident investors and offshore investors, but most offshore dollar bonds are purchased by offshore residents.[33] U.S.-based investors that venture into offshore investments usually do so because they are attracted by the relatively high yields offered by offshore dollar bonds, especially those issued by borrowers in high-growth emerging markets. Offshore dollar bonds give them exposure to that growth without being subject to currency risk.

The offshore dollar capital markets are closely related to offshore dollar banking because the dollars raised

---

[32] Jones, Sam, and Jude Webber. "Argentine Navy Ship Seized in Asset Fight." *Financial Times*, October 3, 2012. https://www.ft.com/content/edb12a4e-0d92-11e2-97a1-00144feabdc0.

[33] He, Dong, and Robert N. McCauley. "Offshore Markets for the Domestic Currency: Monetary and Financial Stability Issues." BIS Working Papers No. 320. BIS, September 2010. https://www.bis.org/publ/work320.htm.

offshore through debt issuance are usually deposited in an offshore bank. For the most part, offshore bond issuers are borrowing dollar deposits held at offshore banks and then depositing them at another offshore bank. The onshore and offshore markets are linked, but most of the offshore activity does not have a U.S.-resident borrower or lender. Offshore banks create dollar deposits as they create dollar loans, and those dollars circulate in the offshore system as payments and investments are made. Some of those investments are in offshore dollar bonds, and the circulation continues.

While most offshore debt issuance is purchased by offshore investors, it's important to note that offshore investors in dollar assets hold most of their dollar investments in onshore securities. Overall, offshore investors hold around $20 trillion in U.S.-based securities.[34] For example, foreign central banks hold around $7 trillion in dollars in their foreign reserves portfolio, which are largely invested in safe U.S. dollar assets such as Treasuries or Agency MBS. The foreign central banks obtained their dollars when their residents exchanged dollars for their home currency or as a byproduct of central bank operations like currency intervention. Institutional investors in Japan and the Eurozone, both regions which have lower interest rates than the U.S., have been increasing investments in U.S.-based assets such as Treasuries, Agency MBS, and corporate bonds.

---

[34] "Foreign Portfolio Holdings of U.S. Securities as of 6/28/2019." U.S. Treasury, April 2020.
https://ticdata.treasury.gov/Publish/shl2019r.pdf.

They usually obtained their dollars through FX-swap loans.

The Dollar as a WMD

The Eurodollar system is offshore, but ultimately, all dollar banking transactions no matter the origin will have a link to the U.S. banking system. After all, off-shore dollars would not really be dollars if they were not fungible with onshore dollars. The U.S. government has authority over the U.S. banking system, and by extension, over the offshore banking system. This implies that the U.S. government has authority over virtually every dollar transaction done through the banking system in the entire world. Let's walk through an example to see how this works.

Suppose a bank in Kazakhstan named KBank has a dollar loan business. KBank makes a $1000 loan to its client and credits its client's account for $1000. The client then withdraws that $1000 to pay a U.S. supplier who banks with a U.S. bank, named UBank. KBank is going to have to settle a payment of $1000 with UBank. There are two ways it can do this: 1) if it has a reserve account at the Fed, then it can send UBank a wire for $1000 in reserves or 2) if it holds its dollars as a bank deposit at a U.S. commercial bank, then it will have to ask that commercial bank to send UBank $1000 in reserves. In the second case, KBank's U.S. commercial bank will send $1000 in reserves to UBank while reducing KBank's deposit balance on its books by $1000. In either example, the transaction must go through the U.S. banking system.

This would be the same even if KBank kept its dollar deposits at a non-U.S. commercial bank and the supplier banked with a non-U.S. commercial bank. Suppose KBank held its dollars as bank deposits at a commercial bank in London and the supplier banked with a commercial bank in Paris. In that case then KBank would ask its London bank to send the supplier's bank in Paris $1000. Assume that the London bank holds its dollars at a U.S. commercial bank, who has a Fed account, and that the Paris bank went through the trouble to open a Fed account, so it did not need to hold its dollars at another commercial bank. Then the London bank will ask its U.S. commercial bank to wire $1000 into the French bank's account, who would then credit the supplier's account. The U.S. commercial bank would send the Paris bank $1000 in reserves. Even though both banks are foreign, the dollar transaction ultimately has to go through the U.S. banking system.

The U.S. government, through its control of the U.S. banking system, has the power to shut anyone out of the dollar banking system. If the U.S. government decides that someone should be sanctioned, then that person will not be able send or receive dollars through commercial banks anywhere in the world. Banks take these sanctions very seriously because if they are caught violating them, then they may also be shut out of the U.S. banking system. That would be a death sentence to any bank. In June of 2014, BNP Paribas admitted to helping Sudan, Iran, and Cuba evade U.S. sanctions and move money through the U.S. banking system. They were forced to pay a breathtaking fine of $9 billion.

In recent years, the U.S. government has shown greater willingness to use its control over dollar payments to further its policies. This is arguably the most powerful nonlethal weapon it possesses as exclusion from the global dollar system would send most into the Stone Age. Iran, who has been sanctioned by the U.S. and the Eurozone, now must sell oil for payment in gold.

The World's Central Bank

Former U.S. Treasury Secretary John Connally famously quipped "the dollar is our currency, but your problem." This remark was made to an audience of shocked foreign officials in 1971 as the U.S. took the dollar off the gold standard. Moving away from the gold standard gave the U.S. greater freedom to run loose fiscal policy, but it also led to significant devaluation of the U.S. dollar. This led to chaos in the global markets, which U.S. officials were not sympathetic to at that time.

U.S. policy makers over the decades have gradually become more sensitive to the impact of the dollar on financial conditions abroad. This may in part be due to the greater interconnectedness of the global economy, where poor economic and financial conditions abroad more easily impact the domestic economy. The existence of a vast offshore dollar system has a couple of key implications: it significantly strengthens the influence of U.S. monetary policy on foreign economies and it significantly raises the risks of financial instability.

The Fed has significant influence on dollar interest rates, and the dollar is used globally, so monetary policy decisions by the Fed have far reaching outcomes. For example, central banks in emerging markets tend to set relatively high interest rates to combat inflation. But if the Fed sets its interest rates at a relatively low level, then emerging market companies will simply borrow in dollars. Dollars are widely accepted and even preferred to some home currencies. In effect, the Fed is wresting some control of monetary policy away from these other central banks.

A large offshore dollar market can potentially be destabilizing because the offshore market participants do not necessarily have the Fed as a lender of last resort as U.S. banks do. If a bank in the U.S. suddenly experiences withdrawals or payments that it can't meet, but is otherwise financially sound, then the bank can borrow from the Fed's discount window. This safety net helps prevent bank runs.

Banks in the Eurodollar system do not necessarily have the same safety net. Foreign banks that have branches in the U.S. will have access to the Fed's discount window, but many foreign banks don't have branches in the U.S. In practice, all large foreign banks have U.S. branches, but smaller ones do not. Applying for and maintaining an account at the Fed is an expensive process that is usually not worth it for a small foreign bank, who will instead hold its dollars as deposits at a large commercial bank. When there is a run on these smaller foreign banks, they go into the wholesale funding markets and start bidding up dollars. This demand for dollars drives up short-term dollar interest rates and destabilizes financial markets.

In times of crisis, the Fed has shown a willingness to lend to foreign banks and support the offshore dollar market. During both the 2008 Financial Crisis and the 2020 COVID-19 panic, the Fed became lender of last resort to foreign banks via the FX-swap lines, where the Fed lends dollars to a foreign central bank, who in turn lends to the foreign banks within their jurisdiction.[35] The Fed feels comfortable doing this because it is lending to a foreign central bank, who is presumably a good credit risk and offering foreign exchange as collateral. The Fed has in effect become the world's central bank and ultimate backer of the dollar banking system.

[35] Aldasoro, Iñaki, Torsten Ehlers, Patrick McGuire, and Goetz von Peter. "Global Banks' Dollar Funding Needs and Central Bank Swap Lines." BIS Bulletin No. 27. BIS, July 16, 2020. https://www.bis.org/publ/bisbull27.htm.

Section II Markets

Chapter 5 – Interest Rates

Interest rates are the building blocks of all asset prices, financial or real. For example, a home buyer takes the mortgage rate into account when deciding how much they are willing to pay for a home, a corporate raider makes a hostile bid for another company based in part on how much their junk bond financing will cost, and an investor takes a stream of cash flows and discounts them with a risk-adjusted interest rate to price a stock. Assets cost money, and interest rates determine how much money costs.

The foundational interest rates for all U.S. dollar assets are Treasury yields, which are the return an investor earns when investing in Treasuries. These returns are considered risk-free, so they form a basis on which all risky investments can be judged. Investors will take a look at how much they can earn by buying Treasuries and then compare that return to what a potential investment is offering. Investors will expect to earn a bit more in a risky investment, with the additional premium increasing with the level of risk. The level of Treasury yields thus has a significant impact on the expected returns from all assets. For example, the level of

Treasury yields will in part determine the level of yield that mortgage and junk bond investors can expect and the discount rates used to arrive at a stock's valuation.

The Treasury issues debt in tenors that range from 1 month to 30 years, and the yields on those securities form the Treasury yield curve. The yield curve tends to be upwards sloping, which means longer-dated yields tend to be higher than shorter-dated yields. The Fed controls short-term interest rates, but long-term interest rates are largely determined by market forces. The level of Treasury yields can have a powerful effect on asset prices, because lower yields imply higher asset price valuations. Analyzing the level of yields and shape of the yield curve can tell us what the market views as the Fed's next action as well as the market's expectation for economic growth and inflation.

Short-term Interest Rates

The Fed controls short-term interest rates through its control over overnight interest rates. In theory, this is through its control of the federal funds rate, which is the rate commercial banks pay to take out an overnight loan for reserves on an unsecured basis. By setting a target range for the federal funds rate, the Fed is able to exert influence throughout the short-term interest curve as market participants use the overnight rate as a reference for what the rate for slightly longer tenors, such as 3 or 6 months, should be. For example, if the Fed set the federal funds rate at around 1% for the foreseeable future, then the interest rate of any 3-month loan is going to have to be at least 1%, otherwise the lender would just lend at 1% overnight every day instead of locking their money into a 3-month investment.

Historically, the Fed controlled the funds rates by controlling the quantity of bank reserves in the banking system. Commercial banks are required by law to hold a certain level of bank reserves against their deposits, and the Fed is the only entity that can create reserves. Each day, the Fed's trading desk would estimate the demand curve for reserves and then adjust the amount of reserves in the banking system needed to maintain the federal funds rate within its target range. However, this method of controlling the federal funds rate became obsolete when the Fed started conducting quantitative easing. Quantitative easing increased the level of bank reserves in the banking system from around $20 billion to a few trillion. It became no longer possible to control the funds rate by adjusting the quantity of reserves.

In the current world with very high levels of reserves, the Fed controls the federal funds rate by adjusting the interest rate it offers on the Reverse Repo Facility (RRP) and the interest it pays on reserves that banks hold in their Fed account. The RRP offers a wide range of market participants the option of lending to the Fed at the RRP offering rate. These market participants include money market funds, primary dealers, commercial banks, and a few government-sponsored enterprises. The option to lend risk-free to the Fed at the RRP offering rate puts a floor on the returns they are willing to accept from the private sector. For example, if an investor can lend risk-free overnight to the Fed at 1%, then it would never be willing to lend at a rate below 1%. The RRP offering rate effectively sets the minimum overnight interest rate in the market. The rate is usually set at the bottom of the Fed's target range to prevent the funds rate from dropping below the range.

The Fed makes sure the federal funds rate stays within its target range by adjusting the interest it pays on reserves. Prior to the crisis the Fed did not pay interest on reserves. The ability to earn interest risk-free from the Fed gives commercial banks a bargaining position when they think about lending or borrowing in the federal funds market. If interest on reserves were 1%, then a bank would only lend reserves if the rates they received were greater than 1%. Otherwise, the bank would just let its reserves sit at the Fed earning that 1%. Some commercial banks are willing to borrow in the funds market, but only at rates below interest on reserves.[36] This is because they can deposit the funds in their Fed account and earn the difference between the funds rate and interest on reserves. Note that at times some commercial banks will perceive federal funds to be a relatively low cost source of funding and borrow even at rates above interest on reserves. These banks can drive

---

[36] Some entities have reserve accounts at the Fed but do not earn interest on reserves. These include Fannie, Freddie, and the Federal Home Loan Banks. Since these entities don't earn any interest on their reserves, they are willing to lend out their reserves at rates below interest on reserves.

the federal funds rate to trade above interest on reserves, but they still look to interest on reserves as a reference rate. The Fed can thus shift the federal funds rate to stay within its target rate by adjusting the interest it pays on reserves. In recent years, the Fed has consistently been able to adjust the federal funds rate by adjusting the interest it pays on bank reserves.

The Fed views its control of the federal funds rate as an essential part of its tool kit and has been willing to go to great lengths to maintain that control. In recent years, the Fed has only lost control of the federal funds rate in one instance: September 17, 2019. On that day there was tremendous volatility in the overnight repo markets, where rates exploded off the charts by doubling to over 5%. Lenders in the federal funds market saw the high rates in the overnight repo market and used that as bargaining power to drive the federal funds rate higher and out of the Fed's target range. In response to this, the Fed restarted quantitative easing and began lending hundreds of billions of dollars in the repo market, which they had not done since the 2008 Financial Crisis. This brought overnight repo rates under control and the federal funds rate back into the target range.

In practice, the RRP offering rate is probably a much more influential rate than the federal funds rate. The RRP rate is available to a wide range of market participants, while the federal funds rate is available only to commercial banks. This means that changes in the RRP rate affect the opportunity costs of a much larger group of market participants. In addition, activity in the funds market has declined significantly since the 2008 Financial Crisis as regulations discouraged commercial banks from borrowing in the funds market, making changes in the funds rate even less impactful on interest rates in the broader market.

The Fed's firm control over overnight rates allows it to exert control along the Treasury yield curve, though its influence declines rapidly as tenors increase. Market participants will use the overnight rate set by the Fed as a reference to value what the 1-week, 1-month, 2-month, etc. Treasury yield should be.[37] Assuming the Fed is not expected to adjust its target range, market participants will expect these short-term risk-free rates to be slightly higher than the overnight risk-free rate; otherwise, the lenders would just lend overnight consecutively while preserving the option of pulling their money back any day they want instead of locking it into a term asset. However, the farther out on the yield curve, the less the current overnight rate matters. This is because the Fed is expected to adjust its overnight rate in the future in line with changes in its economic outlook, so expectations on economic conditions become increasingly important for tenors beyond a few

---

[37] In practice, there are slightly more steps in extending the overnight risk-free rate (RRP rate) to term risk-free rates. The overnight RRP rate influences the overnight Treasury repo rate, which in turn influences term Treasury repo rates, which then affects the pricing of Treasury bills. The RRP is an overnight reverse repo facility with a risk-free counterparty (the Fed), so it directly affects the overnight reverse repo market.

months into the future. Rates beyond the short term are largely determined by the views of market participants.

Longer-Term Interest Rates

While the Fed determines short-term rates, the market determines longer-term interest rates. When an investor is thinking about lending longer term, they take into account a number of things such as how the Fed will set short-term interest rates in the future, estimates for future inflation, how volatile those estimates are, and future supply and demand dynamics of Treasury debt issuance. Since the expected path of the policy rate is just one piece of the puzzle, the Fed has weaker influence on longer-term rates.

A common framework for thinking about longer-term yields is to decompose them into two components: the expectations for the path of short-term interest rates and a term premium. For example, you would expect the returns you could earn on a 10-year Treasury to be equivalent to lending risk-free overnight to the Fed for 10 years plus a premium for keeping your money locked up for 10 years. The first component depends on how the market perceives the Fed to act in the future, which in turn depends on how the market perceives future inflation. Fortunately, there is an easy way to see what the market thinks the future path of policy will be.

The short-term interest-rate futures market offers a glimpse of what the market thinks short-term interest rates will be in the future. The most popular short-term interest-rate future is the market for Eurodollar futures. The Eurodollar futures market is the deepest and most liquid derivatives market in the world. Eurodollar futures are essentially the market's best guess of what future 3-month LIBOR rates will be. Since 3-month rates are firmly within the Fed's control,[38] this is largely a bet as to what the Fed will do in the future, which in turn is a bet based on how economic conditions will unfold.

Of all the financial instruments, Eurodollar futures are the most reflective of economic fundamentals. Eurodollar traders know the Fed will react according to how the economy performs, so they focus on hard economic data even as other asset classes are stuck in moments of euphoria or fear. Often times, they will even disagree with the Fed.

For example, in September 2018, the Fed announced via their "dot plot" projections that they anticipated raising interest rates by 75 basis points in 2019. The Eurodollar futures market saw this and priced in the rate hikes. The Fed slightly lowered their projected rate hikes in 2019 to 50 basis points at their December meeting. This time however, the Eurodollar market instead predicted that the Fed would be cutting rates in 2019. Eurodollar traders may have thought that the large declines in the stock market in December would compel the Fed to change its mind. As is often the case,

---

[38] In practice, LIBOR also contains a credit component. In times of severe market stress, LIBOR can increase even if the Fed does not change its stance of policy. This is because the risks of defaults rise.

the market was correct, and the Fed ended up cutting rates rate three times in 2019.

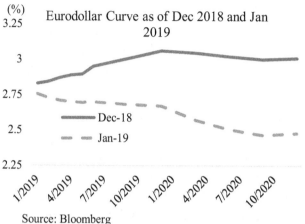

Source: Bloomberg

There are four major Eurodollar futures contracts in each calendar year that take the name of their month of expiry: March, June, September, and December. Each of these contracts is a bet that estimates what the 3-month LIBOR will be at on the contract expiry date of that month. Eurodollars contracts are available for many years into the future, so a market participant can easily see what the market thinks short-term interest rates will be far into the future. For example, the implied rates from the March 2027 Eurodollar contract would be the market's best guess of what the 3-month LIBOR rate will be in March 2027.

Market participants can look at the rates implied by Eurodollar futures to see what the market's best guess is for the path of short-term interest rates.[39] They can then use that as a baseline, compare it to where Treasury yields are currently trading, and derive a term premium.[40] Admittedly, the "term premium" is really just what cannot be explained by the estimated path of short-term interest rates. However, it's not unreasonable to assume that investors would require a term premium to invest in longer-dated Treasuries.

In recent years, the estimated term premium using the Adrian-Crump-Moench model has been historically low, potentially due to lower volatility of inflation in recent years as well as the hedging benefit investors receive from holding Treasuries.[41] In the 1970s and 1980s, inflation was very high and volatile, while inflation during the past 10 years has been very muted. A lower volatility for inflation can make forecasts more precise, thus reducing the level of term premium an investor requires. In addition, the negative correlation between equities and Treasuries has grown stronger in recent years. This makes holding Treasuries valuable as a hedge against stock market declines. Investors may

---

[39] In practice, there is still a spread between 3-month LIBOR and the Federal funds rate that fluctuates over time. To more clearly tease out the expected path of short-term interest rates would require a sophisticated model to account for that spread.

[40] Term premium calculations are complicated and very model dependent. Each model may use different inputs, have different assumptions, and arrive at different values.

[41] Clarida, Richard. "Monetary Policy, Price Stability, and Equilibrium Bond Yields: Success and Consequences." Speech, November 12, 2019. https://www.federalreserve.gov/newsevents/speech/clarida20191112a.htm.

thus be willing to hold Treasuries even at low term premiums.

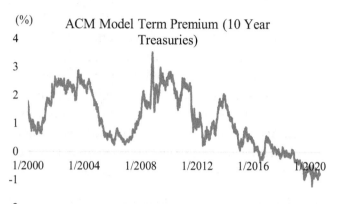

Source: Bloomberg

The discussion above offers a theoretical framework to think about how longer-term interest rates are determined, but basic supply and demand dynamics play an important role as well. Like any other product, increased supply leads to lower prices. When the U.S. Treasury issues more Treasury securities than the market expects, then yields offered by those Treasury securities must increase to attract additional investors. Unfortunately, both supply and demand for Treasuries are difficult to predict.

The supply of Treasuries is determined by the federal government's deficit. When the federal government announces large budget deficits, the Treasury market will usually interpret the news as an increase in Treasury supply, and yields accordingly move slightly higher. The Treasury releases deficit estimates quarterly to help guide investors, but in practice, they are not very useful because deficit levels are ultimately a political decision. Future politicians may adjust spending or taxes in ways that make the forecasts useless. In addition, the Treasury has some flexibility in the tenor of the debt it chooses to issue. Concentrating issuance in the short-dated Treasuries will have limited impact on longer-tenor yields, while issuing in longer tenors will have a direct impact on longer-tenor yields. From time to time, the Treasury will also offer new debt products to fund the federal deficit, most recently, the 20-year Treasury in Q2 2020. All these variables are difficult to predict.

Future demand for Treasuries is just as difficult to estimate as the future supply of Treasuries. This is because Treasuries are purchased by investors throughout the world, with foreign demand in part determined by foreign monetary policies and foreign trade policies. In recent years, negative rates in Japan and the Eurozone have increased demand for U.S. Treasuries, which continue to offer positive returns. The U.S.' chronic trade deficit has led many foreign countries to accumulate a large stock of dollars that they in turn reinvest into Treasuries. China and Japan, two nations with large and persist trade surpluses with the U.S., each hold around $1 trillion in U.S. Treasuries.[42] Changes in trade policy or monetary policy of foreign countries have a meaningful impact on the international demand for Treasuries but are difficult to predict.

---

[42] U.S. Treasury. "Major Foreign Holders of Treasury Securities," https://ticdata.treasury.gov/Publish/mfh.txt.

Domestically, the Federal Reserve is the largest purchaser of Treasuries. The Fed's actions are very difficult to predict because they depend on financial conditions and the judgement of the policy makers at the time. In 2019, many market participants were expecting Treasury yields to rise due to the federal government's growing deficit. When the 2020 COVID-19 panic struck, the Fed decided to purchase over $1 trillion in Treasuries over a span of weeks and committed to purchase large amounts going forward. This essentially solved the demand issue and kept Treasury yields at record lows. The COVID-19 panic, and the Fed's strong reaction, could not have been predicted beforehand. As the Fed becomes increasingly aggressive in its willingness to purchase Treasuries, other factors that affect longer-term yields appear to become less important.

Other than the Fed, major domestic investors include pension funds, insurance companies, commercial banks and mutual funds. These investors are incentivized by regulations to hold low-risk assets such as Treasury securities. For example, Basel III mandates large commercial banks to hold sizable amounts of high-quality liquid assets such as Treasuries. Demand for Treasuries from these domestic investors appears stable but could also change with any modifications to the regulatory framework. For example, regulatory tweaks that allow more risk-taking would dampen demand for Treasuries, which are safe but very low yielding. A looming pension crisis where pensions cannot afford their obligations could conceivably lead to such regulatory tweaks.

Shape of the Curve

In addition to the level of yields, the shape of the yield curve is also an important watch point for investors. The yield curve can be used to infer the market's perception of the state of the economy. Market participants often focus on an inverted yield curve—one where longer-term yields (usually the 10-year Treasury) are lower than short-term yields (usually the 2-year Treasury or 3-month Bill)—as a sign that the economy will soon be in recession.

Recall, longer-term rates are driven in part by the market's expectation of the future path of short-term interest rates. When longer-term interest rates are lower than short-term interest, then the market is expecting the Fed to lower short-term rates soon. That imminent rate cut is already being reflected in the pricing of longer-dated Treasuries. The market thinks the Fed will cut rates soon because it perceives economic weakness that will prompt the Fed to take action. Participants in the bond market are very sophisticated and extremely sensitive to economic conditions, so their judgements are not to be taken lightly. In practice, the market will often, but not always, sniff out economic weakness before the Fed figures out what is happening.

The shape of the yield curve is also in part determined by Fed action. The Fed purchases longer-dated securities through quantitative easing, which effectively lowers longer-term yields and thus flattens the yield curve by putting downward pressure on longer-dated yields.

In the past, the Fed has also engaged in operations which flattened the yield curve by selling short-term Treasuries and buying longer-term ones.[43] This flattens the yield curve by raising short-term interest rates in addition to putting downward pressure on longer-term rates. The size and composition Fed's portfolio can thus impact the shape of the Treasury curve.

Some commentators note that Fed involvement may cause Treasury yields to be less reflective of economic fundamentals. The Fed's share of outstanding Treasury securities is around 20 percent in mid-2020, which is relatively low among major central banks but is gradually increasing. It seems likely that with the great majority of Treasuries outstanding being freely traded, Treasury yields are still sensitive to economic conditions. Even if affected by Fed action, interest rates are still regarded as the best market signal for the state of the underlying economy.

---

[43] This is the Maturity Extension Program, announced September 21, 2011.

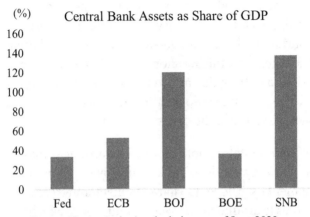

Central Bank Assets as Share of GDP

Source: Haver, Author's calculations, as of June 2020

Chapter 6 – Money Markets

Money markets are markets for short-term loans with maturities that range from overnight to around a year. Money markets are the plumbing of the financial system; they keep the financial system working but are out of sight. The shadow banks and commercial banks are often structured to have longer-tenor illiquid assets funded by short-term liquid liabilities borrowed from the money markets. Without well-functioning money markets, the banks would not be able to operate. When money markets break down, those entities cannot roll over their short-term debt and are forced to sell their assets to repay loans. Historically, breakdowns in money markets have led to fire sales that precipitate into financial crisis.

There are secured and unsecured money markets. In secured money markets, a borrower puts up a financial asset as collateral for a short-term loan. In unsecured money markets, a borrower does not put up collateral and borrows on the basis of their creditworthiness. In the post–2008 Financial Crisis world, new regulations intended to strengthen the financial system led to structural changes that have been unfavorable to unsecured money markets. Basel III discouraged commercial banks from borrowing in unsecured money markets, and Money Market Reform significantly reduced the amount of lending in unsecured money markets. While still sizable, unsecured money markets have correspondingly become less important. Secured money markets appear to increasingly be the money market of choice for borrowers and regulators, with the Fed now publishing secured overnight reference rates and controlling secured overnight rates through ongoing repo operations.

Secured Money Markets

Secured money markets are markets for short-term loans that are secured with financial assets as collateral. Should the borrower default on the loan, then the lender is free to seize the collateral to satisfy the loan. The two largest segments of secured money markets are the repo market and the FX-swap market. Repo loans are secured by securities such as Treasuries, corporate bonds, MBS, or equities. FX-swap loans are loans in one currency secured by another currency, such as a loan for 1000 euros secured by collateral of 1000 U.S. dollars.

In a repo transaction, which is short for repurchase transaction, a borrower "sells" a security to a lender while at the same time entering into an agreement to buy back the same security at a future date at a slightly higher price. The prices for these transactions will be lower than the market value of the security to provide the lender with an extra margin of safety. Economically, this is equivalent to borrowing money using the security as collateral. The slightly higher price paid to repurchase the security is equivalent to the interest on the loan. This transaction structure is advantageous from a bankruptcy law standpoint; even if the borrower files for bankruptcy, the lender will be allowed to seize the collateral because it has technically been sold to them. If the transaction were structured as a secured loan, then the lender would have to go through bankruptcy court before seizing the collateral. In practice, most repo transactions are overnight loans collateralized by safe assets including U.S. Treasuries and Agency MBS.

The repo market is enormous and essential to the modern financial system. The size of the U.S. dollar repo market is not fully known because of data collection limitations, but is estimated to be around $3.4 trillion.[44] The largest segment, overnight loans made against Treasury security collateral, is around $1 trillion each day.[45] U.S. dollar repo transactions are done across the world in all major financial centers. The repo

---

[44] Baklanova, Viktoria, Adam Copeland, and Rebecca McCaughrin. "Reference Guide to U.S. Repo and Securities Lending Markets." Staff Report No. 740. Federal Reserve Bank of New York, December 2015. https://www.newyorkfed.org/medialibrary/media/research/staff_reports/sr740.pdf.
[45] See Federal Reserve Bank of New York. "Secured Overnight Financing Rate," https://apps.newyorkfed.org/markets/autorates/SOFR.

market is used both as a deep source of liquidity and a market for cheap leverage.

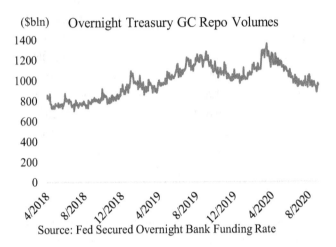

(\$bln)   Overnight Treasury GC Repo Volumes

Source: Fed Secured Overnight Bank Funding Rate

The repo market is the essential link that allows Treasury securities to be "money." The Treasury market is already the world's deepest and most liquid market, but a \$1 trillion overnight repo market goes one step further and allows Treasuries owned outright to be converted to bank deposits any time for virtually no cost, and then returns the same Treasury security the next day. Of course, borrowers can easily roll over their overnight repo loans for as long as they want or choose a longer-tenor repo loan. This makes Treasuries fungible with bank deposits, thus turning Treasuries into money and giving the U.S. Treasury the power of the printing press.

The repo market is also a market for cheap leverage. Investors can speculate on securities by putting down a little of their money as equity and borrowing the rest in the repo market. This is because an investor can purchase a security, simultaneously enter into a repo agreement to borrow against that security, and then pay for the initial purchase of the security using proceeds from the repo loan. For example, a hedge fund who wants to invest $100 in Treasuries can put down $1 of its own money and end up borrowing the remaining $99 in a repo transaction. Here is how that would work:

Step 1: Hedge fund A goes and buys $100 in Treasuries from Hedge fund B.

Step 2: At the same time, Hedge fund A enters into a repo transaction with a dealer where Hedge fund A sells the $100 in Treasuries for $99 dollars and agrees to buy the Treasuries back at $99.01 tomorrow (the $0.01 is the interest for the overnight loan). Hedge fund A cannot sell the Treasuries for the full $100 because the dealer will ask for a small haircut to protect itself from any changes in the collateral value. In this case, the dealer sees Treasuries as very high-quality collateral and is only looking for a 1% haircut.

Step 3: Hedge fund A takes the $99 it received from the dealer, plus $1 of its own money, and pays Hedge fund B $100. Hedge fund A is thus able to buy $100 of Treasuries with just $1 of its own money.

Step 4: The next day Hedge fund A is obligated to purchase the $100 in Treasuries back from the dealer for $99.01, where $0.01 is the interest charged on the overnight loan. Hedge fund A can either renew the loan or get out of the trade by selling the Treasury on the market for $100 and paying the dealer $99.01 with the proceeds.

In practice, a borrower looking for leverage through repo loans could be engaged in a few common strategies: they could be hoping that the security purchased would appreciate, they could be earning interest on the security purchased that is in excess of the interest costs of the repo loan, or they could use the security as a hedge to another part of their portfolio or as part of an arbitrage strategy. In any case, the repo market allows a borrower to take large positions with just a little bit of their own money.

The cash borrowers in the repo market are primarily dealers and the investment funds who borrow from the dealers. Usually a money market fund would lend to a dealer who in turn uses the money to finance their own inventory of securities or acts as an intermediary and re-lends the money to a hedge fund client.

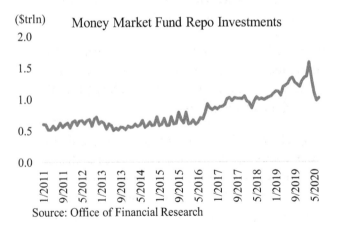

($trln) Money Market Fund Repo Investments

Source: Office of Financial Research

The primary cash lenders in the repo market are money market funds, who lend around $1 trillion dollars each day. Money market funds gravitate towards the repo market because they value liquidity and security. The short maturities of repo loans allow money funds to easily meet investor redemptions, while the high-quality collateral allows them to lend without worrying about default. Money market funds can thus park their money virtually risk-free, earn interest, and have the money back in case there are any investor withdrawals.

In recent years, the Fed has become an active borrower and lender in the repo market through its Repo and Reverse Repo Facilities. The two facilities are used by the Fed to control repo rates. The Fed's Reverse Repo Facility offers money market funds a place to park their money at a set interest rate. This helps the Fed maintain a floor for repo rates because it provides money funds with strong bargaining power against dealers. The Fed's Repo Facility has a similar purpose: it acts to prevent repo rates from rising too much. The Repo Facility provides virtually unlimited repo loans to primary dealers at a set rate, which then acts as a soft ceiling for repo rates. If a money market fund demands rates higher than the Fed's Repo Facility rate, the dealer can just borrow from the Fed instead. The spread between the Reverse Repo Facility rate and Repo Facility rate is usually only a small fraction of a percent.

Deep Dive into the Repo Market

The repo market is the largest and most important market that most people have never heard of. It's about

$3.4 trillion in size and comprised of three major segments: Tri-party, uncleared bilateral, and cleared FICC.[46]

The tri-party repo market refers to trades conducted on the repo platform of a clearing bank, who performs the operational back office work of the transaction such as collateral valuation, securities custody, and payment settlement. Cash lenders in tri-party repo are not specific in the collateral they accept; for example, a lender against Treasury collateral would be open to any tenor Treasury collateral (this is called "General Collateral"). In the U.S., the only tri-party platform is operated by Bank of New York Mellon. Tri-party repo is basically a user-friendly way to conduct repo. As a result, cash lenders like money market funds or corporate treasurers transact the bulk of their repo on a tri-party platform. The cash borrowers in tri-party tend to be dealers who are either financing their inventory securities or borrowing cash to lend to their hedge fund clients. Data from the New York Fed shows that the tri-party repo market is around $2.2 trillion in size.[47]

Cleared FICC repo refers to repo transactions that are centrally cleared through the Fixed Income Clearing

---

[46] A fourth segment, the general collateral financing (GCF) market, has shrunk significantly in recent years and is only around $100 billion. GCF is an interdealer market that is settled in tri-party.

[47] For the latest data, see Federal Reserve Bank of New York. "Tri-Party/GCF Repo," https://www.newyork-fed.org/data-and-statistics/data-visualization/tri-party-repo.

Corporation, a clearing house. The FICC repo market is an interdealer market, so all transactions are between dealers. Dealers in FICC can request specific collateral for their loans; for example, a dealer lending cash can specify that it only wants recently issued Treasury securities. Centrally cleared means that when two dealers agree on a repo trade, they submit the trade to FICC who then takes the other side of the trade to each dealer. If Dealer A agrees to borrow $100 from Dealer B using Treasury securities as collateral, then, through a process called novation, FICC becomes the counterparty facing each dealer. At the end of the trade, Dealer A will be borrowing $100 from FICC, and Dealer B will be lending to FICC. This reduces counterparty risk because FICC is regarded as a high-quality counterparty. It also allows borrowing and lending in FICC repo to be netted since all FICC repo is ultimately with FICC as the counterparty. This helps a dealer's regulatory metrics by reducing its balance sheet size. The FICC repo market is estimated to be a bit over $1 trillion.

Uncleared bilateral refers to repo trades done without the assistance of the tri-party platform and are not novated to FICC. These trades are generally between dealers and either cash lenders that are too small for the tri-party platform or so large that they are able to demand terms more flexible than those possible on the tri-party platform. There is no official data on this segment of the market.

The other major secured money market is the FX-swap market, which is a market for foreign currency loans.

FX-swap transactions are like repo transactions, but instead of securities the collateral used is foreign currency. For example, a 3-month Euro-USD FX swap would be borrowing euros using U.S. dollars as collateral. The party that ends up with dollars will pay a USD interest rate like the 3-month LIBOR and receive a euro interest rate like the 3-month Euribor from the party that ends up with euros.[48] The FX swap allows investors to obtain foreign currency and hedge out exchange risk, which can easily wipe out any investment gains.

The FX-swap market is an enormous market, with estimates of daily volumes around $3.2 trillion.[49] Most of these transactions have the U.S. dollar as one part of the leg. This reflects the preeminent role of the U.S.

---

[48] Technically, a borrower enters in a spot FX transaction to buy foreign currency and simultaneously enters into a forward transaction to sell that foreign currency. The forward rate takes into account the interest rate differential and the basis. In a closely related instrument, the FX basis swap, the two parties would exchange currency amounts, make ongoing interest payments to each other that include the basis (if any), and then return the same currency amounts at the end of the transaction. FX-swaps and FX basis swaps are economically equivalent. For more information, see Baba, Naohiko, Frank Packer, and Teppei Nagono. "The Basic Mechanics of FX Swaps and Cross-Currency Basis Swaps." *BIS Quarterly Review*, March 2008, 82.
https://www.bis.org/publ/qtrpdf/r_qt0803z.htm.

[49] "Triennial Central Bank Survey of Foreign Exchange and Over-the-Counter (OTC) Derivatives Markets in 2019." BIS, 2019. https://www.bis.org/statistics/rpfx19.htm.

dollar in the world, where both foreign corporations and foreign investors have strong dollar needs. Foreign companies need dollars to conduct international trade, and foreign investors need dollars to invest in U.S. assets. Lenders of U.S. dollars in the FX-swap market tend to be domestic commercial banks, U.S. investors who seek to invest in foreign assets, or foreign central banks seeking to earn a return on their dollar reserves.

In recent years, U.S. interest rates have been higher than the rest of the developing world. As Japan and the Eurozone moved their policy rates negative, U.S. rates remained positive. Negative rates have made investing difficult for Japan and Eurozone investors and pushed many of them to search for yield outside of their respective countries. However, any foreign investment can only make sense if the currency risk is hedged. For example, suppose U.S. Treasuries yielded 2% more than Japanese government bonds. While 2% is a hefty difference when it comes to interest rates, a 2% move in the yen/dollar currency cross is a relatively frequent occurrence. Thus, while a Japanese investor could earn a higher return in Treasuries, they could easily lose all that and more if the yen suddenly appreciated. An FX swap allows the Japanese investor to hedge out currency risk but at a price that may not always make sense. In addition to paying a USD interest rate, the foreign investor usually also has to pay a "basis."

FX-swap markets are subject to supply and demand dynamics like any other market, and this dynamic is expressed in the "basis" of a FX swap. Following the example above, if there is stronger demand in the market for dollars than yen, then the yen lender will have to offer more than just 3-month USD LIBOR to entice dollar lenders. This extra interest, called the "basis," is determined by the market and is a good barometer of global demand for dollars. Foreign investors looking to invest in U.S. dollar assets will usually look at the returns after accounting for FX hedging costs, which may be sizable enough to make higher-yielding U.S. dollar investments unattractive. Note that the yen lender would pay USD interest on their dollar loan and receive yen interest on the yen lent. In negative interest countries like Japan, the yen lender would be receiving negative interest on the yen lent, which is to say they would be paying interest both on the dollar loan and on the yen lent. Generally, the FX-swap basis for dollars with major currency pairs is a fraction of a percent. But in times of stress it can be much higher. During the 2020 COVID-19 panic, demand for dollars pushed the basis to around 1.5%, where borrowers of dollars had to pay 3-month USD LIBOR plus 1.5%.

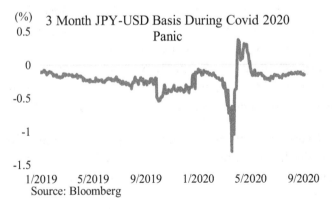

3 Month JPY-USD Basis During Covid 2020 Panic

Source: Bloomberg

During the 2008 Financial Crisis and the 2020 COVID-19 panic, the FX-swap basis for major dollar crosses exploded from a fraction of a percent to several times that in a matter of weeks.[50] This implies significant stress in the U.S. dollar funding markets because borrowers are unable to borrow dollars unless they offer exceptional interest rates. This could happen as U.S. dollar holders pull back their FX-swap lending to conserve dollars and reduce risk amidst market turmoil. When the dollar lenders pull back, foreign investors who borrowed dollars in the FX-swap market on a short-term basis to purchase longer-term U.S. dollar assets may be forced to sell those assets at fire sale prices. Foreign banks with a U.S. dollar loan business and who manage their currency risk through the FX-swap market may be forced to rollover their FX-swap loans at very high rates, leading to significant capital losses that cause them to retrench from lending activity. All this causes significant stress in the financial markets.

In both crises, the FX-swaps market was calmed only when the Fed stepped in and offered to enter into FX-swap transactions with other major central banks. The Fed would lend dollars to a foreign central bank secured by foreign central bank reserves, and the foreign central bank would then lend those dollars to banks

---

[50] Coffey, Niall, Warren B Hrung, Hoai-Luu Nguyen, and Asani Sarkar. "The Global Financial Crisis and Offshore Dollar Markets." *Federal Reserve Bank of New York Current Issues in Economics and Finance* 15, no. 6 (2009). https://www.newyorkfed.org/research/current_issues/ci15-6.html.

within its jurisdiction. These actions were effective in calming the FX-swaps market during both crises, but it took several hundred billion dollars of emergency swap loans.

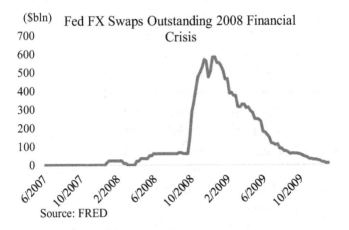

Source: FRED

Money Markets are Global

Sophisticated investors often view money markets as a global market where they can freely move around the world in search of the highest return. They will look at the interest rates offered by money market products throughout the world, taking account of FX hedging costs. For example, even when Eurozone sovereigns issue short-term debt at below zero percent, a U.S.-based investor can still find it more attractive than positive-yielding short-term Treasury securities after taking FX hedging costs into consideration.

Market Pricing in December 2019	
3M U.S. Treasury Bill	1.5%
3M French Bill	-0.6%
3M EUR LIBOR	-0.4%
3M USD LIBOR	1.9%
3M EUR/USD FX-swap basis	0.2%

In late 2019, 3-month French bills yielded -0.6% while 3-month Treasury bills yielded 1.5%. On its face, a U.S. investor could earn much more investing in the 3-month Treasury bill than a 3-month French bill (1.5% vs -0.6%). But that was not the case on a FX hedged basis. If the investor swapped their dollars into euros and then invested into the 3-month French bill, then they would have earned 3M USD LIBOR by lending dollars, paid negative 3M EUR LIBOR for euros (which means receiving positive interest), received the FX-swap basis, but lost 0.6% in negative yielding French bills. Overall, they would be earning 1.9% (1.9% + 0.4% + 0.2% - 0.6% = 1.9%), which is 0.4% more than Treasury bills over the same period.

Focusing solely on domestic interest rates can be misleading because money markets are global. Changes in interest rates in one country automatically affect those in other countries via arbitrage. Not all investors can participate in the arbitrage due to varying levels of sophistication and risk tolerance, so the opportunities persist.

Unsecured Money Markets

Unsecured money markets are markets for short-term loans where the promise to repay is backed by nothing other than confidence in the borrower. These loans tend to offer higher interest rates than secured loans because of the higher risk involved. While a secured lender would lend largely on the quality of the collateral backing the loan, unsecured lenders rely heavily on ratings agencies to determine the creditworthiness of a borrower. Common unsecured money market instruments include certificates of deposit, commercial paper, and federal funds. In the post-2008-crisis world, unsecured money markets have become less important as regulations discouraged banks from borrowing in them.

Before the 2008 Financial Crisis, commercial banks were major participants in the unsecured money markets. The well-known benchmark rate, 3-month LIBOR, is in fact a benchmark rate for the interest rate a commercial bank would have to pay to borrow dollars on an unsecured basis for 3 months. Borrowing in unsecured money markets was an easy way for a commercial bank to expand its loan portfolio without worrying about deposit outflow. When a commercial bank aggressively expands its loan portfolio, it will often experience net deposit outflows as the newly created deposits are spent by borrowers and end up deposited at other commercial banks. In this case, a commercial bank could go to the market even when they don't have collateral and borrow in the unsecured money markets to replace the lost deposits.

The largest segment of unsecured money markets are certificates of deposit (CDs), which are essentially deposits that cannot be withdrawn until they reach a preset maturity date. While data on CDs is not publicly available, Federal Reserve data show that commercial bank time deposits were around $1.6 trillion in 2020. Time deposits are a slightly broader category of bank liabilities that include CDs. These deposits offer banks a way to manage outflows, and depositors a way to earn competitive interest rates. The largest issuers of CDs tend to be foreign banks, as they lack the stable retail deposit base that domestic commercials banks have. Retail deposits can be withdrawn any time, but in practice tend to just sit in the bank. Domestic banks have an easier time managing their deposit outflows because most of their deposits are stable retail deposits. Foreign banks don't have retail businesses, so they have to instead rely on CDs where the depositor is contractually obligated to keep the deposit at the issuing bank until the CD matures.

Investors in CDs tend be very rate sensitive. These investors will quickly move money from one bank to another even for a fraction of a percent. The largest investors in CDs are prime money market funds, who usually invest in CDs issued by a number of commercial banks as a way to diversify credit risk. Because CDs are unsecured, many investors are reluctant to put large sums of money into a single bank's CDs. Instead, investors would invest in prime money market funds and benefit from the fund's diversification.

Another common unsecured money market instrument is commercial paper (CP). Whereas CDs are legally deposits and can only be issued by commercial banks, CPs are short-term unsecured debt that are not deposits, so they can be issued by any entity. When a financial institution issues CP, it is called financial CP. Insurance companies, bank holding companies, dealers, and specialty finance companies are all common issuers of financial CP. Many non-financial corporations also actively issue CP to manage their working capital, such as vendor payments, payroll, inventory management, etc. Non-financial CP is a relatively small portion of unsecured money markets. This helps non-financial CP issuers borrow at slightly lower rates than financial CP issuers, even controlling for credit rating. Investors in non-financial CP are willing to accept slightly lower returns to diversify their portfolios away from financial issues. Prime money market funds are the dominant investors in CP, as they are in CD.

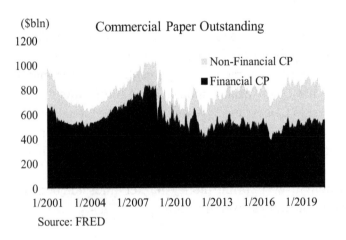

Commercial Paper Outstanding

Source: FRED

Money Market Reform 2016

An earthquake shook the money market world on October 14, 2016, when a few long-awaited money market reforms came into effect. First announced by the SEC in 2014, the reforms were designed to make money funds safer in light of the failure of a few prime money market funds during the financial crisis. One of the major changes was to give prime money market funds the option to freeze redemptions in times of market stress. This was designed to prevent a run on prime money market funds, where massive investor flight would force the fund to liquidate assets at fire sale prices and result in investor losses.

Prime fund investors were terrified of the possibility of having their money frozen in a prime fund when they would need it most. Many investors in prime funds were institutional investors who in turn were managing someone else's money. If these institutional investors could not redeem their prime fund investments, then they might not have the cash on hand to meet their own redemptions. That possibility was too terrifying for many institutional investors, and they decided to move their money en masse out of prime funds and into government funds, which did not have the redemption gate feature. As the October 14, 2016 effective date approached, prime funds lost a record $1 trillion dollars in assets over the span of a few weeks.

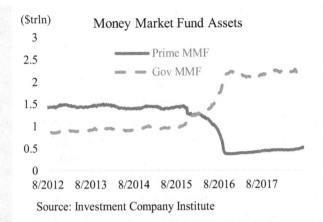

($trln) Money Market Fund Assets

Source: Investment Company Institute

Prime funds were the dominant investors in the unsecured money markets, as government money market funds cannot invest in unsecured private sector liabilities. This meant that in the span of a few weeks, borrowers that had relied upon unsecured money markets would lose close to a trillion dollars in funding. The largest borrowers in unsecured money markets were foreign banks. Heading into October, the 3-month LIBOR rocketed to multiyear highs as foreign banks competed for the remaining prime fund investments. On the flipside, government money market funds were flooded with money and were forced to place hundreds of billions into the Fed's RRP facility because they had nowhere else to invest.

Source: Bloomberg

Money market reform led to dislocations in the unsecured money markets, but the market quickly sorted things out. Over the next few months, the banking sector was able to adapt to the seismic shift in funding sources by adjusting the way that it borrowed. Foreign banks who were accustomed to issuing CDs to prime funds would now instead borrow from government funds through the repo market. Government funds were able to lend in the repo market if the loan was secured by Treasury or Agency MBS collateral. The banking sector essentially rewired itself from large-scale unsecured borrowing to large-scale secured borrowing using Treasuries or Agency MBS as collateral.

The most well-known unsecured money market is the federal funds market, which is where the Fed sets its policy rate. The federal funds market is an interbank market where commercial banks borrow reserves from each other on an overnight unsecured basis. Historically, commercial banks borrowed in the funds market to have enough reserves to meet reserve requirements at the end of the day or to meet daily payment needs. In a sense, it was the marginal cost of funding for a commercial bank. The Fed hoped to influence longer-term interest rates and bank lending activity by raising or lowering the federal funds rate.

The Fed was able to control the funds market because it had complete control over the supply of reserves in the banking system, and a very good sense of the demand for reserves. The demand for reserves came from the regulatory framework that commercial banks operated under, which forced them to hold certain levels of reserves depending on their size and the types of liabilities they had. The Fed knew exactly how much reserves the commercial banking system as a whole needed and adjusted the supply of reserves so that the funds rate stayed within the target range. As is discussed in Chapter 5, the Fed now controls the funds rate with a new framework.

While unsecured markets remain sizable, they are much smaller than they were prior to the financial crisis. The financial crisis was fundamentally a banking sector crisis, and that experience left many market participants, including banks, wary of unsecured exposure to banks. Regulators have also put forth rules that make it unattractive for a bank to borrow in the unsecured money markets. As a result, the interbank unsecured money markets have virtually disappeared. What remains of the unsecured money markets is primarily a nonbank to bank market, and that has also shrunk significantly due to Money Market Reform.

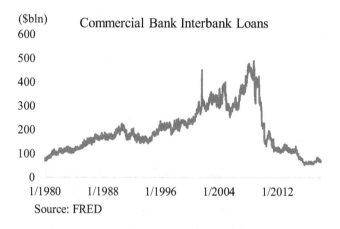

(\$bln) Commercial Bank Interbank Loans

Source: FRED

The Death of the Federal Funds Market

Even though the federal funds market continues to be where the Fed sets its policy rate, the funds market died many years ago. Before the 2008 Financial Crisis, the funds market was deep and dynamic, with hundreds of billions of dollars exchanged each day. Commercial banks borrowed and lent funds in it throughout the day as they adjusted their liquidity positions. The funds rate was relatively volatile as it reflected dynamic market conditions. Note that this is in part because the funds rate was a weighted average prior to March 2016, but a median afterwards.

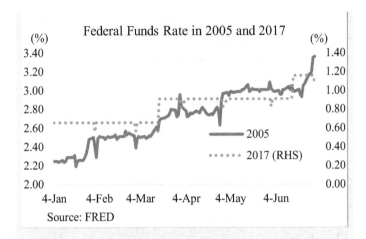

Federal Funds Rate in 2005 and 2017

Source: FRED

In the post-financial-crisis world, the federal funds rates is basically unchanged each day, like an EKG meter that has flatlined. This is due to two reasons: quantitative easing and Basel III. Quantitative easing significantly increased the level of central bank reserves in the banking system from about $20 billion to a few trillion. Commercial banks have much less of a reason to borrow in the funds market when they already have so many reserves. In addition, Basel III made interbank borrowing less attractive. When a crisis hits, those loans are usually the first to disappear and leave a bank scrambling for cash, so Basel III seeks to make commercial banks safer by encouraging them to reduce their overnight unsecured borrowing.

The funds market today exists largely due to a quirk in regulations. Federal Home Loan Banks (FHLBs) have reserve accounts at the Fed, but they are not eligible for interest on reserves. To earn at least a little bit of interest on their reserves, FHLBs lend into the funds market. Some foreign banks, who are more lightly regulated than domestic banks, are willing to borrow from FHLBs and then deposit the funds into their Fed account to earn the interest on reserves rate. They thus earn the small spread between the rate they borrowed at and the Fed's interest on reserves rate.

As the funds market has largely lost its significance as a signal for funding conditions, the Fed is likely to move its target rate to other reference rates. This could be one of the Fed's new references rates such as Secured Overnight Funding Rate (SOFR), which is a reference rate based on overnight repo transactions secured by Treasury collateral. SOFR captures a market that is around $1 trillion in size with a wide range of market participants, so it is much more representative of real funding market conditions. In addition, the Fed already has good control over the overnight repo market through its Reverse Repo and Repo facilities.

Joseph Wang

Chapter 7 – Capital Markets

Capital markets are where borrowers go to borrow from investors rather than from commercial banks. The borrowings are usually at tenors of several years, which put the borrowings outside of money markets. Capital markets financing is different from a commercial bank loan in that it does not increase the amount of bank deposits in the system, but allows holders of bank deposits to lend them to other nonbanks.[51] In a sense, it allows a more efficient use of existing money by allocating it to the borrowers who value it the most. Capital markets are broadly divided into equity and debt markets. Equity markets are where a company offers an ownership interest in itself in exchange for bank deposits. Debt

---

[51] Commercial banks are also able to participate in capital markets but are not major players. When a commercial bank lends in capital markets it takes an asset onto its balance sheet and credits the bank account of the borrower with bank deposits. This is the same as a bank-originated loan. Commercial banks occasionally issue equity and debt securities on behalf of themselves that essentially reduce the aggregate level of bank deposits by transforming some of the bank deposits into equity or debt. Commercial bank borrowing in the capital markets thus reduces the amount of money in the banking system.

markets are where a borrower offers an "IOU" in exchange for bank deposits to be repaid with interest at an agreed upon date.

Equity Markets

Equity markets are the most followed financial market by the public. Major equity indices like the Dow Jones are talked about on the news and often viewed as a barometer for the health of the overall economy. However, equity markets are actually the most emotional market and least reflective of economic conditions. An easy way to see this is to see how often equity markets go into manias where they swing higher, only to crash over a short period of time even as the underlying economic data has not materially changed.

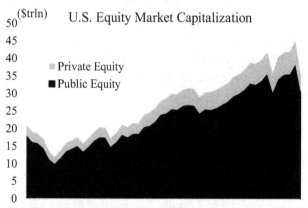

U.S. Equity Market Capitalization

Source: Federal Reserve Z1

Market participants generally try to value equities on either a fundamental or relative level. Fundamental analysts will take a discounted cash flow approach and view a stock price as a series of future earnings discounted by a risk-adjusted discount rate. After forecasting future earnings and then determining a discount rate, the fundamental analyst will arrive at a valuation. An analyst valuing a stock on a relative basis would compare it to similar stocks. For example, a shoe company's stock could be considered expensive if its price to earnings ratio or some other valuation metric were higher than another comparable shoe company's ratio. Relative valuation can also be conducted across asset classes, such as comparing the returns of Treasury securities to the expected future returns of a stock.

The difficulty with using valuation to predict the future price of a stock is that there are many ways of valuing a stock and it is not clear that one method is consistently better than others. Prior research has suggested that stocks that are "cheap" on a price to book ratio tend to outperform, but more recent research suggests that may no longer be true.[52]

---

[52] For a discussion on value premium see Fama, Eugene F., and Kenneth R. French. "Common Risk Factors in the Returns on Stocks and Bonds." *Journal of Financial Economics* 33, no. 1 (1993): 3–56. https://doi.org/10.1016/0304-405X(93)90023-5. For a discussion on how changes in market structure have affected the value premium, see Green, Mike, and Wayne Himelsein. "Talking Your Book About Value (Part 1)."

The Rise of Passive Investment

The structure of the equity market has changed significantly over the past couple decades due to the rise of passive investment.[53] More and more Americans are investing in the stock market through employer-sponsored retirement plans such as target date funds that don't invest according to valuations the way an active investor would. While an active investor would buy stocks according to some sort of valuation metric, a passive investor does not care about the price. For example, retirements funds will invest the money allocated to them each paycheck period, no matter how expensive stock valuations are. Over the past two decades flows from passive investors have grown to become the marginal investors in the equity market. This has a few extremely important implications:

- The stock market trends higher. Every week there is a constant flow of new money entering the stock market, even if valuations are considered to be sky high. This creates an upward bias in the market as a whole.
- Stocks with large market capitalizations continue to get even bigger at an accelerating rate. Retirement accounts are usually set to track a certain stock index, like the S&P 500. Companies with larger market capitalizations in an index are allocated a greater share of money by index tracking funds,

Logica Capital, May 14, 2020. http://fedguy.com/wp-content/uploads/2021/12/Talking-Your-Book-on-Value.pdf.
[53] For more information, see the work of Mike Green at Simplify Asset Management.

which in turn pushes the price of the stock higher. This is because a stock's order book depth, which represents the amount and size of the outstanding buy and sell orders, does not scale perfectly with the market cap of the stock, so the increased investment flows into large cap stocks push their prices upwards at an accelerating rate. As the price of a stock rises, it becomes a bigger part of an index and so more money needs to be allocated to it, reinforcing the upward momentum. In a market dominated by passive investment, companies with large market caps become even bigger. This is exactly what is seen in the incredible outperformance of large cap tech companies like Microsoft or Apple. Not coincidentally, the two companies happen to be members of all three major equity indexes: the Dow Jones, S&P 500, and Nasdaq.

- Value investing no longer works. Value investing relies on the idea that "cheap" companies tend to appreciate over time and outperform the market. This was famously documented by the Fama-French study that used price to book value as a measure of value. However, that study was done in a world before passive investment flows dominated the market. Cheap companies, which tend to be smaller companies, are largely absent from the major stock indices that receive passive investor flows. These value companies thus continue to underperform. The active investors that look for value cannot compete with the constant torrent of retirement money that drives major stock indices higher.

Many market participants believe in the existence of a "central bank put" where significant declines in major equity market indices will compel central banks to do something to push market prices higher. No central bank official will ever acknowledge such a policy, but that is exactly how major central banks around the world have acted in the past decade. In November 2010, Chair Bernanke, in defense of a new round of quantitative easing, noted that higher stock prices created a wealth effect that could improve consumer sentiment and thus consumer spending.[54] The Fed believed that higher stock prices could help them achieve their policy goals. The stock market had appeared to become a policy tool.

In 2014, the Bank of Japan became the first major central bank to begin purchasing equities. Japanese stock market indices were euphoric and surged higher in the months following the announcement, but then drifted around in the following years. Of course, many aspects other than central bank actions affect equity prices, and many notable events transpired in the following years, but Japanese stock market indices appeared to be less and less excited by subsequent announcements of additional BOJ equity purchases. The Nikkei essentially traded sideways from 2015 to 2020 even as the BOJ steadily increased its ownership of Japanese equities to around 6% of the market capitalization of the Tokyo Stock Exchange.

---

[54] Bernanke, Ben. "Aiding the Economy: What the Fed Did and Why." Op-ed. Board of Governors of the Federal Reserve System, November 5, 2010. https://www.federalreserve.gov/newsevents/other/o_bernanke20101105a.htm

The Fed does not have the legal right to purchase equities. However, the Fed has been creative in finding ways to support the financial markets in times of crisis. Recent history shows a clear pattern of the Fed taking on riskier assets onto its balance sheet, so it is not inconceivable that one day the Fed could purchase equities.

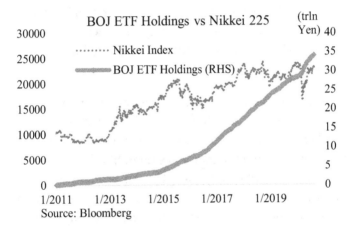

BOJ ETF Holdings vs Nikkei 225

.... Nikkei Index

BOJ ETF Holdings (RHS)

Source: Bloomberg

The equity market is more than just the stocks listed on an exchange. There also exists a separate market for non–publicly traded private equity. To be able to sell equity shares to the public, a company goes through a regulatory process and then finally launches an initial public offering (IPO). It is then subject to ongoing regulatory disclosures and must respond to the interests of its new shareholders, who may have a wide range of conflicting visions for the company. While an IPO gives a company the opportunity to raise money from a large pool of investors, some companies decide that it isn't worth the trouble, preferring instead to look to the private markets to raise money.

Companies can raise money through private markets by offering equity for sale to accredited investors, who are investors that meet a certain regulatory standard of wealth or sophistication. These investors are assumed to not need the regulatory protections that an IPO offers because they are sophisticated enough to conduct their own due diligence. Companies who choose to not list their equity publicly are generally smaller and less sophisticated than their public counterparts. For example, a medium-sized family-owned business may seek to raise money by selling shares in the company to institutional investors. The institutional investor buys an ownership interest in the business and sometimes offers some managerial expertise to further improve the business.

There are some benefits for a company to remain private, even if it can IPO. Often, remaining private allows the company to be more long term in its thinking because its shareholders also have a longer time horizon. Public companies are under a quarterly reporting cycle and may be forced to behave in ways that maximize short-term gain at the expense of longer-term profitability. Owners of public companies also run the risk of losing control in a hostile takeover, as anyone can go out and purchase enough shares of the company to gain control.

Private equity investments can potentially yield high returns, but on average appear to have returns comparable to the broader stock market.[55] Private equity investors further suffer a serious liquidity problem. Investors in public equity can easily sell their shares on an exchange, but there is no exchange for private equity. Investors looking to sell their private equity shares must look for other sophisticated investors, provide confidential financial information on the company to help the buyer evaluate the investment, and then agree on a price. On the bright side, the lack of a liquid market allows private equity investors to avoid marking down their holdings even if public equity markets crash.

The illiquidity problem frequently leads private companies on the path to becoming public companies. An IPO offers an easy way for the private equity holders to cash out. Founders and investors in private companies may have enormous wealth based on model valuations of their private equity holdings, but all their wealth is only hypothetical unless they can actually sell the shares. Once the shares are publicly traded, they can easily monetize their holdings by logging onto an online brokerage and selling at the price that is flashing on the screen.

Market Makers: An Invisible Hand

Equity prices usually exhibit a pattern of a slow grinding move upwards, punctuated by sudden large drops.

---

[55] Barber, Felix, and Michael Goold. "The Strategic Secret of Private Equity." *Harvard Business Review*, September 2007. https://hbr.org/2007/09/the-strategic-secret-of-private-equity.

There is always a shifting array of explanations for these drops, but one is the structure of the equity markets. Institutional investors tend to buy puts to hedge their downside and sell calls to generate additional income. Options dealers usually take the other side of these trades. As a result, options dealers are forced to hedge their options book in a way that slows down upward moves in equity prices but accelerates downward moves.

An options dealer makes money from transaction fees it earns from selling and buying options. It does not take a directional view as to whether stocks will go up or down; it is only interested in earning a transaction fee. For example, when an investor wants to sell a call option on a stock, the dealer will take the other side of the bet and end up owning a call option. If the stock price goes up, then the value of the call will increase. As the dealer's business model is based on transaction fees instead of directional bets, the dealer will hedge its exposure to the call option by shorting the stock. This way, when the stock price goes up, the dealer's gain on the call option is offset by its short (this is called being "delta hedged"). If the stock price declines, then the value of the call will also decline. To remain delta hedged, the dealer will reduce its short stock position by buying some of the stock. As dealers are structurally long call options, the higher the stock goes the more shares the dealer shorts, and the lower the stock goes, the more the dealer buys. This moderates the rate in which stock prices rise and decline.

However, dealers also tend to be structurally short puts. This is because investment funds buy puts to insure their portfolios. When a dealer is short a put a different dynamic occurs. To hedge a short put position, the dealer sells stocks. This way, when stock prices decline the dealer is losing money on its short put position but earning money on its short stock position. The lower stock prices go, the more shares the dealer has to sell to remain hedged. If stock prices increase, then the value of the short put also increases. This leads a dealer to reduce its short stock position by buying shares, which reinforces the upward movement in stock prices. This dynamic enables a volatile self-reinforcing cycle of stock prices that can lead to sudden stock market crashes and sudden upward surges in stock prices.

When a dealer is short an option, whether it is a put or call, the dealer is "short gamma." That means that its losses on the put (call) it sold will increase in a nonlinear fashion as the price of the underlying stock declines (rises). This forces the dealer to sell (buy) ever increasing amounts of the underlying stock to hedge its position as the price of the stock is decreasing (increasing). On the other hand, when a dealer is long an option, the dealer is "long gamma." They hedge their position in the opposite direction of the price move, so they sell (buy) shares of the underlying stock when the price is increasing (decreasing). Hedging a short gamma position reinforces the price trend, while hedging a long gamma position moderates the price trend.

The amount of hedging the dealer community does is estimated to be in the billions for even small moves in the S&P 500.[56] Dealers are usually long gamma, but sudden drops in the equity market occur can push their out-of-the-money puts into the money and require additional hedging. This means sudden declines in the level of equity indices can push dealers into short gamma and force them to sell large amounts of stocks to remain hedged, further exacerbating downward price moves. That pattern is exactly what we see in real life.

Debt Capital Markets

Debt capital markets are less glamorous than equity markets, but larger and arguably more important. These are where companies or governments borrow money by issuing bonds. A bond is just a promise to re-pay issued by a borrower in exchange for an investor's bank deposits. When a commercial bank originates a loan, it creates bank deposits that are credited to the borrower's bank account, but when a nonbank bor-rower issues a bond to a nonbank investor, then the nonbank investor sends bank deposits to the nonbank borrower's account. Rather than create more bank de-posit money, the debt capital markets allow a more effi-cient use of existing bank deposit money.[57]

---

[56] See www.squeezemetrics.com for daily estimates of dealer gamma positioning.
[57] Commercial banks can still be involved in the debt capi-tal markets by borrowing or lending. In the former case it essentially transforms bank deposit liabilities into longer-

The bond markets are a lot more complicated than the equity markets because bonds are highly customizable along many dimensions. For example, they come with all sorts of tenors, interest rates, seniority, optionality, and covenants. Any big company will likely have just one kind of stock publicly listed on the stock exchange, but it will certainly have several issues of debt outstanding. Some of it could be long term, some short term; some could be floating rate, some fixed rate; some could be senior unsecured, some secured; some could be callable, etc. Even Treasury securities come in a wide range of tenors and coupons. This makes understanding the bond market a very complicated undertaking.

The bond market is also opaquer than the stock market. While stocks are identified by a ticker symbol that is usually four or fewer alphabetic characters, bond issues are identified with a CUSIP[58] number that is a nine-character alphanumeric identifier. For example, "91282CAE1" is the CUSIP for the 10-year Treasury maturing August 2030. Anyone can search on the internet to find the price a stock is trading at, but searching for the price of a specific CUSIP often requires access to professional platforms. Furthermore, most bonds don't

---

term debt, which helps it manage its outflows. In the latter, it is functionally the same as making a bank loan. When a commercial bank purchases a bond, it credits the sellers account with freshly created bank deposits. The main difference between a bond and a loan is that bonds are readily tradable, so they are much more liquid.

[58] CUSIP is an acronym for the "Committee on Uniform Securities Identification Procedures," the group that manages these numbers.

trade frequently, so you may not have any data on its price unless you call a dealer.

Market participants usually evaluate bonds in terms of their yields as a spread to Treasury yields of the same tenor. For example, a 5-year bond issued by Microsoft would be evaluated by how much additional yield it offers over 5-year Treasuries. Treasuries are assumed to be risk-free and highly liquid. The additional yield offered by the Microsoft bond is meant to compensate an investor for the credit and liquidity risk the investor is taking.

Credit risk takes into account how likely the company will default, and if it does, what percentage of the money lent could be recovered. Credit ratings are the single most important determinant of a bond's perceived credit risk. Large investors do not realistically have the time to carefully go through the financials of every company they invest in, so they place a lot of reliance on ratings agencies to do the work. In many cases, reliance on ratings is literally written in their mandate, where they can only invest in bonds that are above a certain rating. The higher a company is rated, the lower the interest rate they can borrow at. Once a company's rating falls below investment grade, the interest rates it can borrow at shoot up significantly because many investment funds are not allowed to purchase so-called junk bonds.

Liquidity risk takes into account how difficult it would be to sell the bond in case the investor needed money before it matured. While Treasury securities trade throughout the world and around the clock, most other bonds trade infrequently. Depending on market conditions, an investor may not be able to sell their bond without a significant discount. A bond's spread over Treasury securities is wider when the bond is more illiquid.

The bond market is generally thought of as the "smarter" market because it is more sensitive to economic fundamentals. A bond investor only cares about being able receive their investment back plus interest, while an equity investor can dream of the unlimited upside offered by a company's next product. Bond investors don't have any upside beyond principal and interest payments, but they can lose money if a company is unable to repay its debts. Deteriorations in a company's fundamentals will quickly be reflected in the company's bond prices, but not necessarily in its equity prices.

The general public is aware and actively engaged in the stock market, but much less aware of the intricates of the bond market. For example, after Hertz filed for bankruptcy in June 2020, its bonds quickly traded down to pennies on the dollar, reflecting the low likelihood of any recovery. In bankruptcy, all debt holders are paid in full before equity holders receive anything, so a bankruptcy filing almost always implies that the company's equity is worthless. However, Hertz's stock surged after bankruptcy as an army of retail investors piled in. These investors were likely unaware of the implications of a bankruptcy filing, which was quickly understood by the bond holders.

Source: Bloomberg

The bond market is segmented into different sub-classes, the largest of which are Treasury securities, mortgage-backed securities, and corporate debt. Other notable segments are municipal bonds and asset-backed securities. The sections below will offer a broad overview of the three largest segments of the bond market.

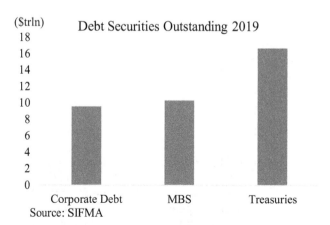

Source: SIFMA

Corporate Bonds

Corporate bonds are held by a wide range of investors, the largest of which are insurance companies, pension funds, and mutual funds. A small but increasingly important investor class are ETF funds. Broadly speaking, the market is divided into an investment-grade universe (bonds rated BBB-[59] and above) and a high-yield universe (bonds rated below BBB-, also known as junk bonds). According to S&P, around 85% of corporate bonds are investment grade and the rest are high yield. Insurance companies and pensions funds tend to be more conservative in their investments, so their corporate bond holdings are largely investment grade, while mutual funds ETFs vary significantly according to their investment strategies. Mutual funds and ETFs that offer high yields will have a higher composition of high-yield bonds.

---

[59] These are under S&P ratings, which rates credit from highest to lowest as AAA, AA, A, BBB, BB, B, and CCC, with an added plus or minus as in-between ratings. The two other credit ratings agencies, Moody's and Fitch, have comparable ratings systems. In practice, all three major agencies usually give an issuer equivalent ratings.

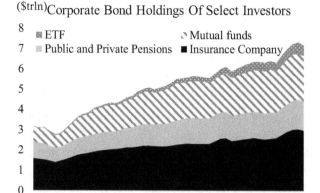

($trln)Corporate Bond Holdings Of Select Investors

Source: Federal Reserve Z1, also includes foreign bonds

While a relatively small holder of corporate bonds, ETFs have grown in prominence as a source of liquidity and price discovery for the corporate bond universe. Corporate bond ETFs hold a diversified portfolio of corporate bonds but issue shares that are traded actively throughout the day like a stock. The shares are much more liquid than any of the underlying corporate bonds, so how the shares trade give a real time glimpse as to how the fund's portfolio of bonds is being valued. The relationship between share value and the underlying corporate bond assets of the ETF is policed through arbitrage. Institutional investors are also able to sell baskets of their corporate bonds to the ETF in exchange for shares of the ETF or redeem ETF shares for baskets of corporate bonds.

Borrowers in the investment-grade corporate bond market tend to be larger corporations with solid credit ratings. In recent years, the investment-grade corporate bond market has grown tremendously as interest rates and corporate bond spreads reached record lows. The highest rated corporate issuers can borrow billions at yields that are only slightly above inflation and much lower than what any commercial bank can offer. This is because a bank would price a loan not just on credit risk, but would also take into account the effect the loan has on its regulatory ratios and return on equity. Corporate bond investors do not have these concerns but focus on the relative returns of comparable products such as Treasuries or Agency MBS. As central bank policy has reduced the yields on comparable products, corporate bond investors have been forced to accept lower and lower yields on their bond investments.

Borrowers in the high-yield market tend to be corporations with high debt levels relative to their cash flow, thus explaining their lower credit ratings. They are generally former investment-grade companies that had been downgraded or younger companies that lack the operational history required for an investment-grade rating. In the high-yield space, commercial banks can offer a comparable product called leveraged loans, which are essentially high-interest loans. Being a loan, leveraged loans are not as easily tradable as high-yield bonds and may also come with more restrictions on how the money can be used. These restrictions, called covenants, would be enforced through ongoing monitoring by the bank. In practice, banks often originate and then sell the leveraged loans into a Collateralized Loan Obligation (CLO) investment vehicle, which then securitizes the loans. The bank will retain only the highest rated senior bonds of the CLO and the rest will go to investors with higher risk appetites.[60]

Just as many market participants are convinced of the existence of central bank "put" on the equity market, some market participants are also becoming increasing confident of a central bank "put" on the debt markets. This is because central banks are becoming increasingly active buyers in the corporate debt market.

The BOJ was the first major central bank to begin buying corporate bonds in 2013, followed by the ECB in 2016 and finally the Fed in 2020. These purchases were justified based on improving the transmission of monetary policy by lowering the borrowing costs of corporate borrowers, thus stimulating the economy. Instead of relying on low rates to be transmitted to borrowers through the banking system, the central bank can now directly lower the borrowing costs of corporations by buying corporate bonds and thus pushing yields lower. Corporate bond purchases by central banks do appear to lower corporate borrowing costs, but also appear to make corporate bonds less sensitive to economic fundamentals. Many market participants now are less concerned with their risk exposure to corporate debt as

---

[60] DeMarco, Laurie, Emily Liu, and Tim Schmidt-Eisenlohr. "Who Owns U.S. CLO Securities? An Update by Tranche." FED Notes. Board of Governors of the Federal Reserve System, June 25, 2020. https://www.federalreserve.gov/econres/notes/feds-notes/who-owns-us-clo-securities-an-update-by-tranche-20200625.htm.

they believe the central banks will just keep bond prices high even when fundamentals deteriorate.

Source: Bloomberg, Federal Reserve H4 Table 4

In practice, the amount of corporate bonds purchased by central banks has been relatively small. The Fed's purchases have been a particularly small 0.1% of the U.S. corporate bond universe. Like many other central bank policies, it appears that the perception that the central bank is in the market is sufficient to boost investor confidence. Market participants may simply expect the Fed to massively increase its purchases in the event of financial distress.

How QE Lifts Stocks: Corporate Leveraging

A corporation can finance itself using equity or debt. Equity holders are the owners of the corporation, so they share in the risk of the enterprise. If the company is very profitable, then the equity becomes more valuable, and if the company goes bankrupt, then the equity holders receive nothing. In contrast, the debt holders get paid their principal and interest and nothing more. If the company goes bankrupt, then its assets are sold off and the proceeds go to the debt holders.

One of the ways in which a corporation can boost its equity prices is by issuing debt to buy back equity. Suppose that equity holders, because they are subject to more risk, demand a 10% return on their equity. At the same time, because interest rates are low, the same company can issue debt at 5%. Then, by issuing debt to buy back stock, the corporation reduces its cost of capital. The company is effectively borrowing at 5% to repay 10% obligations. At the same time, there will be fewer shares of stock outstanding so each shareholder would receive more of the earnings. This leads to higher stock prices purely through financial engineering.

Over the past few years, quantitative easing has helped push longer-term interest rates to record lows. Corporations have taken advantage of the record low interest rates and issued record amounts of debt that they used to buy back stock. A notable example of this is Apple, which bought back around 20% of its shares between 2015 and 2019.[61] Even though the company's net income in 2019 was around the same level as in 2015, its earnings per share had materially risen due to the

---

[61] Santoli, Michael. "Apple's Stock Gains the Last 4 Years Prove 'Financial Engineering' via Buybacks Works." CNBC, July 31, 2019. https://www.cnbc.com/2019/07/31/santoli-apples-gains-are-largely-the-product-of-buyback-financial-engineering.html.

smaller number of shares outstanding. This financial engineering helped Apple's share prices double over that 4-year period.

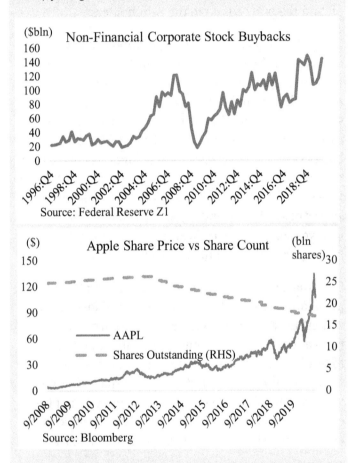

However, there are also clear risks to an increase in corporate leverage. While there are fewer shareholders to share the profits with, there are also fewer shareholders to share the losses with. In the event of an economic downturn, shareholders will experience higher losses per share, which may result in large declines in share prices. A more highly leveraged capital structure suggests greater volatility in stock prices on both the upside and downside.

Agency MBS

Agency MBS are mortgage-backed securities guaranteed by the government. Mortgage-backed securities are bonds that receive the cash flow generated by a pool of mortgage loans. The government can either guarantee the mortgage-backed securities or the mortgage loans underlying those securities. Agency MBS are the second largest market for bonds in the U.S., with over $8.5 trillion outstanding. The vast majority of Agency MBS are backed by single family home mortgages, with around a $1 trillion backed by commercial real estate mortgages that are predominately multifamily homes. Agency MBS have minimal credit risk,[62] are very liquid, and have returns that are slightly higher than Treasuries, so they are very popular with conservative investors like insurance companies and foreign central banks worldwide. Around $1 trillion in Agency MBS are held

---

[62] Agency MBS guaranteed by Ginnie Mae have no credit risk because Ginnie Mae is a part of the federal government. Agency MBS issued by Fannie and Freddie benefit from an implicit government guarantee. While they are not part of the federal government, it is assumed that they are backed by the federal government. This assumption was tested during the 2008 Financial Crisis and proved true when the federal government provided its full support to Fannie and Freddie as they became insolvent.

by foreigners, with over 60% of that held by Asian investors.[63]

Fannie Mae and Freddie Mac

Fannie and Freddie are the two giants of the mortgage bond market. Their job is to support the U.S. housing market by providing liquidity in the secondary mortgage market. They do this by buying mortgage loans and packaging them into securities that can be sold to investors. The loans underlying the securities are guaranteed by Fannie and Freddie, so investors don't have to worry about any homeowner defaulting.

Historically, mortgages were originated by commercial banks who held on to the mortgage loans for interest income. Fannie and Freddie offer commercial banks the additional option of selling the mortgage loan, provided the loan meets certain minimal credit standards. This additional flexibility was designed to encourage commercial banks to make more mortgage loans since they always had the option of selling them to Fannie or Freddie in case they needed to raise money. This created a robust secondary market for mortgage loans and also made possible an "originate to distribute" business model where mortgage loans were primarily originated to be sold rather than held as investments.

---

[63] Kaul, Karan, and Laurie Goodman. "Foreign Ownership of Agency MBS." Ginnie Mae, July 2019. https://www.ginniemae.gov/newsroom/publications/Documents/foreign_ownership_mbs.pdf.

Today, most mortgage loans are originated by nonbank mortgage lenders who specialize in the "originate to distribute" business model.[64] These mortgage lenders take out a loan from a commercial bank, lend the money to a home buyer, sell the mortgage to Fannie or Freddie, and then repeat the process by taking the proceeds from the sale and lending to another mortgage borrower. Nonbank mortgage lenders make money off the origination fees, not the interest from the loan. In the early 2000s, this volume-driven business model led to a lowering of lending standards as lenders tried to maximize the volume of loans originated, but post-crisis regulations have significantly clamped down on that kind of behavior.

Fannie and Freddie take the mortgage loans, add a guarantee onto them, package them into securities, and return them to the mortgage seller to be sold to investors. A guarantee from Fannie and Freddie make the mortgage securities virtually risk-free. Should a mortgage loan default, Fannie or Freddie will buy it back so the investors would not face any losses. These securities, called Agency MBS, are in significant demand worldwide because they offer slightly higher yields than comparable Treasuries with minimal credit risk. This demand for Agency MBS creates more demand for mortgage loans, which in turn encourages more

---

[64] Shoemaker, Kayla. "Trends in Mortgage Origination and Servicing: Nonbanks in the Post-Crisis Period." *FDIC Quarterly* 13, no. 4 (2019): 51–69.

mortgage origination, which makes more mortgage loans more widely available to the public.

Prior to the 2008 Financial Crisis, Fannie and Freddie were very profitable businesses since they collected guarantee fees while house prices marched upward relentlessly. When house prices crashed in 2008, Fannie and Freddie had guaranteed around half of all the mortgage loans in the U.S. The mass foreclosures following the crash quickly made Fannie and Freddie insolvent and compelled a government rescue. Since then Fannie and Freddie have remained in government conservatorship.

Agency MBS bonds are a bit tricky to evaluate because mortgage borrowers have the option of prepaying their mortgage. Treasuries cannot be prepaid, and corporate borrowers issuing bonds with prepayment options usually don't exercise them. Prepayments means an investor doesn't know for sure when they will be paid back. An investor who purchased a 30-year Agency MBS might get their money back in 25 years if interest rates fell and large numbers of mortgage borrowers decided to refinance their mortgages. When a mortgage is refinanced, a new mortgage loan is taken out to repay the old mortgage loan, so the mortgage investor gets paid back sooner. On the other hand, if an investor purchased a 30-year Agency MBS on the assumption that prepayments would remain steady, but in fact, interest rates rose and prepayments declined as fewer borrowers refinanced, then the investor will get paid back later than they expect. Prepayment uncertainty means that any valuation of an Agency MBS is model dependent. Investors will try to estimate future prepayments and then discount the cashflows to produce a valuation.

The Fed has been an active buyer in the Agency MBS market since the 2008 Financial Crisis with the stated objective of supporting the housing market and placing downwards pressure on interest rates. The Fed's holdings as of September 2020 were a sizable $1.9 trillion, around 20% of all Agency MBS outstanding. By purchasing large quantities of Agency MBS, the Fed encourages mortgage lending by increasing the resale value of mortgage loans. Mortgage lenders usually sell the mortgage loans they originate to investors, who hold them through Agency MBS. When prices for Agency MBS are high, mortgage lenders are incentivized to increase lending, even at lower interest rates, because they can resell the loans at higher prices to Agency MBS investors.

That One Time When the Private Sector Created Risk-free Assets

When the U.S. Treasury issues Treasury debt, it's as good as any form of money. It's risk-free and can easily be sold or put up as collateral for cash in the repo market. There was also a time when the private sector could do something like that, back in the early 2000s.

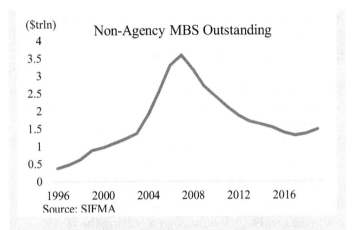

($trln) Non-Agency MBS Outstanding
Source: SIFMA

In the early 2000s, there was a booming market for securitized private-label mortgage-backed securities. A private-label MBS is a bond that is backed by mortgages that are not guaranteed by a government-sponsored enterprise like Fannie Mae. Instead, they could be loans made to borrowers who have very low credit scores or no documentable income. Financial engineers would take these mortgages and create reportedly risk-free securities through credit enhancement techniques like subordination and overcollateralization.

For example, suppose $1000 worth of low-quality mortgages are backing $900 worth of securities. Further, suppose that the $900 worth of securities were divided into three tranches: a $100 A tranche, a $300 B tranche, and a $500 C tranche. Using subordination, any cashflow from the mortgages would first be directed to pay off the $100 A tranche, then the $300 B tranche, then the $500 C tranche. The subordination of the B and C tranche to the A tranche lowers the risk of default for the A tranche. With overcollateralization, $1000 of collateral is used to back $900 of bonds, which means that $100 of mortgages can default before any of the bonds take losses. Taken together, the A tranche would only take losses if $900 of collateral defaulted. This is unlikely and makes the A tranche very safe.

Ratings agencies also took the view that such large defaults were unlikely and often rated these senior tranches as AAA, which made them as safe as U.S. Treasuries but with higher yields. Investors snapped them up, and a large and liquid market for them developed. They became money.

However, when housing prices began declining in 2006, investors began to feel less confident in the quality of the mortgages backing their securities. Many of the subordinate private-label MBS tranches began to trade at discounts. In early 2007, Bear Stearns, a major investment bank, failed because too many of its investments in private-label MBS soured. Investors began to suspect that even the AAA-rated tranches were not safe and began dumping them. Many investors and banks took enormous losses, which eventually precipitated the 2008 Financial Crisis.

In retrospect, almost all of those AAA-rated tranches were paid off.[65] Investors who bought them in 2008

---

[65] Ospina, Juan, and Harald Uhlig. "Mortgage-Backed Securities and the Financial Crisis of 2008: A Post Mortem." BFI Working Paper 2018-24. Becker Friedman Institute, April 2018. http://dx.doi.org/10.2139/ssrn.3159552.

during the financial crisis easily doubled their money in a few years. However, the damage had been done, and the private-label MBS market never recovered. Furthermore, regulators decided that safe assets must be created by the public sector and even AAA-rated private sector assets could not be considered safe. Today, when regulated entities are required to hold high-quality liquid assets, that exclusively means government assets.

Treasury Securities

Treasury securities are the deepest and most liquid market in the world and the bedrock of the global financial system. Almost all U.S. dollar assets are priced off of Treasury yields, which are considered the risk-free benchmark. While retail investors hold bank deposits as money, institutional investors throughout the world hold Treasuries as money. They pledge Treasuries as collateral to purchase other financial assets, borrow against them in the repo market for immediate cash, or sell them outright for cash. Treasuries are issued by the U.S. government in regular auctions in a range of tenors, broadly divided into bills and coupons. Treasury bills are short-term debt that matures within 1 year and is issued on a discount basis,[66] while coupons are issued

---

[66] Discount basis means that it is sold for less than face value. For example, if a 1-month bill is sold at 99 cents then that means the buyer will receive $1 upon repayment in a month. In effect, they will earn 1 cent in a month, which annualizes to an annual interest rate of about 12%.

in tenors that range from 2 years to 30 years and pay interest semi-annually.

The stated debt management strategy of the U.S. Treasury is to issue at regular and predictable times at the lowest long-term cost to the taxpayer. [67] In practice, this means that the Treasury will issue coupons in predictable sizes and make up funding shortfalls with bill issuance. For example, if the Treasury announced $100 billion in coupon issuance for the quarter but then realized it needed $20 billion more, then it would just issue $20 billion more in bills. Coupons are auctioned monthly in sizes that are announced at the beginning of each quarter, while bills are auctioned twice weekly in flexible sizes. If Treasury needed to further customize its cash flow needs, it could issue Cash Management Bills, which are essentially bills that are issued in a nonstandard tenor.

The Treasury bill market is very deep and can easily absorb significant fluctuations in issuance. Investors have little concern holding these as short-term debt, as it is essentially money that pays interest. In contrast, the market values of longer-dated Treasuries can fluctuate with expectations of inflation and interest rates and can become less liquid over time. The most recent issue of coupons is called "on the run," while coupons issued from previous auctions are called "off the run." On-the-run coupons are very liquid, but become progressively

---

[67] For more information see "Overview of Treasury's Office of Debt Management." https://home.treasury.gov/system/files/276/Debt-Management-Overview.pdf.

less liquid as time goes on. An owner of a deep off-the-run coupon can still instantly borrow cash against the coupon in the repo market, but would have more trouble selling it outright. This makes investors of coupons a bit more cautious, so while bills can be elastically sold, coupon supply sticks to a schedule.

Treasury debt is auctioned by the New York Fed to primary dealers, who then resell the debt to their clients. Technically, investors can place bids through the primary dealers (indirect bid), or investors can go through the process of becoming eligible to bid directly themselves (direct bid). Notwithstanding that, primary dealers play a key role in the auction process because they are obligated to bid on every auction. This means an auction can never fail due to lack of demand because it is backstopped by the primary dealers.

The success of an auction can be judged by the auction award rate and degree of participation. A very successful auction would be one where the yield awarded is lower than the yield anticipated by the market and the amount of bids submitted far exceeds the amount of Treasuries being auctioned (high bid to cover). A relatively low share of purchases by primary dealers also suggests strong investor demand. Auction results help the market gauge the demand for Treasuries and can thus move prices. Results that are very strong or very weak often lead to discrete moves in Treasury yields as investors reevaluate their view of pricing in light of the new information. Auction results are released publicly on the Treasury's website right after each auction.

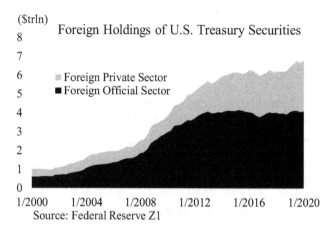

($trln)
Foreign Holdings of U.S. Treasury Securities

- Foreign Private Sector
- Foreign Official Sector

Source: Federal Reserve Z1

Treasuries have a global investor base, with around $7 trillion held by foreigners. This is in part due to the dollar's role as the world's reserve currency. Central banks around the world must hold dollar reserves to facilitate currency exchange or defend their currency against significant depreciation. They tend to hold their dollar reserves in the form of Treasuries. For example, China is estimated to hold around $3 trillion foreign reserves with a sizable share of it in Treasuries. This is not out of the goodness of their heart, but out of self-interest. China runs a large, persistent trade surplus with the U.S., so over time, it accumulates large amounts of dollars. It needs to keep those dollars to participate in global trade, such as purchasing industrial commodities like oil. A large institutional investor like the People's Bank of China (PBOC) simply doesn't have any investment options for dollars other than Treasuries. Private sector assets have credit risk and are not deep enough to hold all that money. If the PBOC had sizable holdings of corporate debt or equities, they would only be able to sell their holdings slowly unless they accepted deep discounts. Treasuries, and to some extent Agency MBS, are their best options.

Notwithstanding significant foreign holdings, most Treasuries continue to be held by domestic investors. Money market funds are major investors in bills, while mutual funds, insurance companies, and pension funds are major investors in coupon Treasuries.

The Fed has been the single largest buyer of Treasuries since the beginning of quantitative easing in 2008. The stated purpose of the purchases was to stimulate the economy by lowering medium- and longer-dated Treasury yields, which the Fed otherwise did not have much control over. Since all assets are in part priced off of Treasury yields, lowering these yields leads to lower mortgage rates, auto rates, commercial loan rates, etc. As of September 2020, the Fed has increased its share of the Treasury market to 20%. This clearly exerts downward pressure on Treasury yields, but likely still leaves room for price discovery.

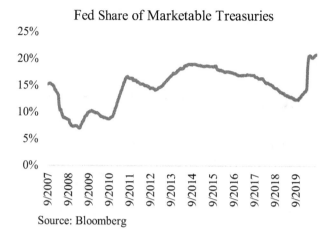

Fed Share of Marketable Treasuries

Source: Bloomberg

Section III Fed Watching

Chapter 8 – Crisis Monetary Policy

Conventional monetary policy relies on the central bank to be the lender of last resort to commercial banks and to use short-term interest rates to influence economic activity. When a financially sound bank suddenly has outflows that it has trouble meeting, the central bank would step in and lend in order to prevent a panic. When the economy is in recession, the central bank would lower interest rates to encourage consumption and investment, and when the economy overheats, it would raise interest rates to tamp down on economic activity.

But what happens when there is a panic in the shadow banking system, and how can a central bank influence economic activity when interest rates are already at 0%? These were the challenges faced by the Fed during the 2008 Financial Crisis and 2020 COVID-19 panic. In response, the Fed devised a new series of tools.

Democratizing the Fed

The Fed was established in an era where commercial banks were the dominant players in the financial system, so its attention was naturally focused on the commercial banking sector. The Fed regulates domestic commercial banks to ensure they are prudently run and offers them emergency loans through the discount window to meet unexpected liquidity needs. However, the growth of shadow banks and offshore banking meant that a significant amount of financial activity now takes place outside of the Fed's purview. In 2008, panics emerged in the shadow banking and offshore banking world. To save the financial system, the Fed was forced to use its emergency Section 13(3) lending powers, which essentially allow the Fed to lend to anyone.

In 2008, the shadow banking world was falling apart. There was a run on the primary dealers, there was a run on the money market funds, there was a run on the securitization vehicles, and there was a run on the hedge funds. The commercial banks were not safe either, because they were deeply intertwined with the shadow banks. They had guaranteed many obligations of the shadow banks and had also lent them a lot of money. The stock market indices sensed the trouble and were imploding. A collapse of the entire financial system was on the horizon.

The Fed met the crisis by vastly expanding its lending counterparties to include key shadow banking sectors. It set up lending facilities for the primary dealers (Primary Dealer Credit Facility), for money market funds (Money Market Investor Liquidity Facility), and securitization vehicles (Asset-Backed Commercial Paper and Term Auction Securitization Facility) and even special loans for too-big-to-fail banks. The Fed effectively became the lender of last resort not just to the commercial banks, but also to the shadow banks.

A similar crisis was playing out outside the U.S. in the offshore dollar banking system. Just as U.S. commercial banks and shadow banks were imploding from the losses on subprime mortgage-related investments, foreign commercial banks were also in crisis for the same investments. The European banks had notably made huge investments in U.S. mortgage-related assets and were potentially insolvent from the losses. However, foreign banks were even further removed from the Fed's purview as they were not even in the U.S. It would be poor optics for the Fed to bail out foreign banks. Yet their impact on U.S. markets was undeniable as their desperate bid for cash pushed dollar short-term interest rates to dizzying heights.

Market participants usually measure stress in short-term interest-rate markets with the spread between the benchmark market rate of 3-Month LIBOR and the 3-Month Overnight Index Swap, which is roughly the expected average federal funds rate for the next 3 months. When the spread is wide, that means that market rates are much higher than the Fed's policy rate, which suggests financial distress. In benign times, the spread is a bit higher than zero, but in the depths of the financial crisis, it reached all-time highs of around 4%. Investors were afraid to lend to foreign banks, forcing the foreign banks to offer extremely high interest rates for even 3-month loans.

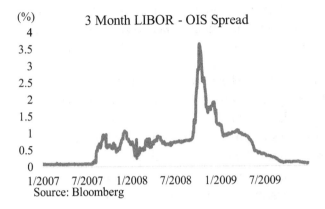

Source: Bloomberg

The Fed ultimately decided to lend to foreign banks by establishing central bank swap lines with a roster of friendly foreign central banks. The Fed would lend dollars to a foreign central bank, who in turn would lend to the banks within their jurisdiction. The swap lines solved the global dollar bank run, but they also essentially made the Fed the backer of the global dollar system, both within and outside of the U.S.

How to Monitor Fed Special Lending Facilities

The Fed discloses its balance sheet on a weekly basis via the H.4.1 release on its website. The values are weekly averages and Wednesday snapshots. Below is a snapshot of the H.4.1 on July 2, 2020.

Repurchase agreements (6)	75,379	+	2,250	+	75,379	61,201
Foreign official	144	+	144	+	144	1,001
Others	75,236	+	2,107	+	75,236	60,200
Loans	96,886	+	2,928	+	96,785	97,133
Primary credit	5,877	-	1,246	+	5,859	5,860
Secondary credit	0		0		0	0
Seasonal credit	13	+	1	-	70	16
Primary Dealer Credit Facility	2,616	-	1,364	+	2,616	2,486
Money Market Mutual Fund Liquidity Facility	21,617	-	1,851	+	21,617	20,637
Paycheck Protection Program Liquidity Facility	66,763	+	7,389	+	66,763	68,113
Other credit extensions	0		0		0	0
Net portfolio holdings of Commercial Paper Funding Facility II LLC (7)	12,799	+	2	+	12,799	12,799
Net portfolio holdings of Corporate Credit Facilities LLC (7)	41,359	+	1,403	+	41,359	41,940
Net portfolio holdings of MS Facilities LLC (Main Street Lending Program) (7)	37,502	+	4,822	+	37,502	37,502
Net portfolio holdings of Municipal Liquidity Facility LLC (7)	16,080	+	1	+	16,080	16,081
Net portfolio holdings of TALF II LLC (7)	8,753	+	1,467	+	8,753	8,753
Float	-497	-	314	+	104	-756
Central bank liquidity swaps (8)	226,803	-	49,894	+	226,786	225,414

From the release, you can see the size of all the major Fed lending programs implemented during the COVID-19 panic. The data show that the emergency credit facilities were little used, with the largest utilizations at $75 billion in repo loans and $66.7 billion via the Paycheck Protection Program Liquidity Facility. In some situations, the mere existence of a Fed credit facility can calm the markets and thus restore market functioning. Market participants know that the Fed is backstopping the market, so there is less tail risk. The lack of usage itself doesn't necessarily mean that the emergency facilities were not needed or had no effect.

One notable exception is the FX-swap lines. The Fed's FX-swap lines were heavily drawn upon, with $226 billion outstanding on that date. A more detailed breakdown of Fed swap-line usage can be found on the New York Fed's website, which reveals the Bank of Japan to be the major user of FX swaps. This is not unexpected, as Japanese investors have very large holdings of USD assets that they fund through the FX-swap market. They are thus most likely to need emergency funding in the event of a disruption in USD money markets.

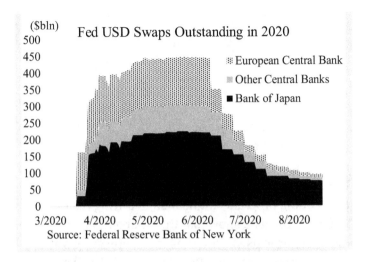

Fed USD Swaps Outstanding in 2020

($bln)

■ European Central Bank
■ Other Central Banks
■ Bank of Japan

Source: Federal Reserve Bank of New York

The end result of these actions was stabilization of the financial system and the establishment of a precedent where the Fed would be the lender of last resort for commercial banks, shadow banks, and even foreign banks. During the 2020 COVID-19 panic, this precedent was even more firmly established as the Fed promptly rolled out virtually all the 2008 crisis-era 13(3) facilities. They even went one step further and took upon themselves the responsibility of being the lender of last resort to private businesses.

In March and April of 2020, the Fed announced new facilities that were targeted at lending to small businesses through commercial banks and larger businesses through the capital markets.[68] The Primary and

---

[68] "Federal Reserve Announces Extensive New Measures to Support the Economy." Press Release. Board of Governors of the Federal Reserve System, March 23, 2020.

Secondary Corporate Facilities would buy corporate bonds in the primary and secondary market, while the Main Street Lending Facility offered to buy eligible loans that commercial banks had made to small businesses. The Fed had firmly stepped beyond its traditional role of offering liquidity to commercial banks, to offering liquidity to virtually all of America's businesses. They had democratized access to their balance sheet to virtually everyone but individuals.

One common critique to the Fed's expansion of lending powers is moral hazard, which is when someone acts recklessly because they know they are insulated from the consequences. During the 2008 crisis, many commentators suggested that bailing out investors who made poor decisions would encourage more poor decision-making, because now investors would think that the Fed would be there to bail them out. This thinking contributed to the decision to allow investment bank Lehman Brothers to fail. The failure of Lehman Brothers precipitated declines in financial assets that were so terrifying that even those afraid of moral hazard no longer stood in the way.

The Fed chose to address moral hazard in another way: regulation. In the aftermath of the crisis, the Fed and

---

https://www.federalreserve.gov/newsevents/pressreleases/monetary20200323b.htm; "Federal Reserve Takes Additional Actions to Provide up to $2.3 Trillion in Loans to Support the Economy." Press Release. Board of Governors of the Federal Reserve System, April 9, 2020. https://www.federalreserve.gov/newsevents/pressreleases/monetary20200409a.htm.

regulators across the world enacted much more stringent regulation on banks such that they would be unable to undertake the levels of risk they had before. Therefore, the banks would unlikely ever need another Fed bailout. These reforms appear to have been successful, as domestic commercial banks sailed through the COVID-19 panic with little issue.

New regulations were also used to reform major shadow banks like the primary dealers and money market funds. These sectors also sailed through the COVID-19 panic with ease, with only the prime money market funds experiencing some trouble. However, other shadow banks like mREITs, ETFs, and private investment funds were not subject to enhanced regulation. Many of these entities suffered large losses during the COVID-19 panic and were only saved by Fed actions.

Reaching Across the Curve

In 2008, the Fed reached the zero lower bound, where the overnight interest rate is 0%, which on its face seemed like a point where monetary policy would become powerless as the Fed could no longer lower interest rates. But the Fed was able to surprise everyone with the introduction of two new tools: forward guidance and quantitative easing.

Forward guidance is a way for the Fed to extend its control of interest rates from short-term rates to medium-term rates as well. The Fed would verbally commit to keep its policy rate low for an extended period of time. As long as the market believed in the Fed's commitment, then even medium-term interest rates should move lower as the market would price out any rate hikes from the present to medium term. The interest-rate curve during a recession is usually upwards sloping with 2-year Treasuries at higher yields than the overnight policy rate. This is because the market expects that the economy will gradually rebound and prompt the Fed to raise its policy rates, so overnight rates in the future will be higher than they are today. Under forward guidance, the curve becomes much flatter because the Fed is committing to keeping its policy rate low even if the economy recovers.

In June 2019, the Treasury curve was inverted, suggesting a near-term recession in which the Fed would soon cut overnight rates, leading to a steeper curve. A year later, the recession arrived and the curve both steepened and flattened. Chair Powell said in his June 2020 press conference, "we're not even thinking about thinking about raising rates."[69] The market priced out any rate hikes for the next few years.

---

[69] Powell, Jerome. "Transcript of Chair Powell's Press Conference." Press Conference. Board of Governors of the Federal Reserve System, June 10, 2020. https://www.federalreserve.gov/mediacenter/files/FOMCpresconf20200610.pdf.

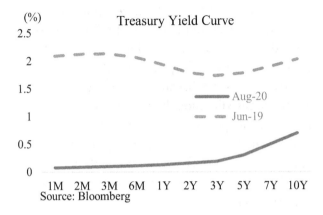

(%) Treasury Yield Curve

Aug-20

Jun-19

1M 2M 3M 6M 1Y 2Y 3Y 5Y 7Y 10Y

Source: Bloomberg

There are different ways that the Fed can implement forward guidance. It can do so by committing to keeping rates low until specific economic performance targets are met or for specific lengths of time. For example, the Fed can commit to keeping interest rates at zero until inflation rises sustainably above 2%, until the unemployment rate drops below 4%, or for a minimum of 2 years, etc. In the aftermath of the 2008 crisis, the Fed has used both types of guidance, initially relying on lengths of time and then relying more on economic targets. Forward guidance appeared to be well understood by the market, but it also appeared to lead to more volatility around important data releases as market participants directly linked movement towards economic targets with Fed action.

Quantitative easing is a way for the Fed to control longer-term interest rates by purchasing longer-dated Treasury bonds and thus driving the yields of those bonds lower. When it was first announced, quantitative easing understandably generated an enormous amount of controversy. Many feared imminent hyperinflation, and the price of gold skyrocketed. Obviously, hyperinflation did not occur. Purchasing Treasury securities by printing central bank reserves was like printing a $100 bill and using it to buy another $100 bill. The amount of money in the system didn't change, just the composition of it. There were now fewer Treasury securities and more central bank reserves.

Research conducted by the Fed suggests that quantitative easing was effective in lowering longer-term interest rates, which helped stimulate economic activity.[70] Even without research, basic supply and demand dynamics suggests that buying trillions in Treasury securities would exert upward pressure on their price (downward pressure on yields). However, quantitative easing also did not appear to have significant side effects. After over a decade of use, the Fed has become comfortable with quantitative easing and deployed it in size during the COVID-19 panic.

Both forward guidance and quantitative easing have moved from unconventional to conventional parts of the Fed's toolkit after over a decade of use. They have both proven effective in influencing the level of interest rates. In 2020, the Fed has also begun preliminary

---

[70] Kim, Kyungmin, Thomas Laubach, and Min Wei. "Macroeconomic Effects of Large-Scale Asset Purchases: New Evidence." Finance and Economics Discussion Series 2020-047. Washington: Board of Governors of the Federal Reserve System, March 2020. https://doi.org/10.17016/FEDS.2020.047.

discussions of yield curve control (YCC), which would potentially allow even more precise control of interest rates. YCC is when a central bank announces specific numeric targets for its interest rates. Note that YCC was actually first used during World War II when the Fed sought to support the war by keeping interest rates low. Interest-rate control under YCC is likely to require fewer central bank bond purchases as market participants know the central bank is willing and able to enforce its expressed interest-rate target with unlimited purchases.

Yield curve control is one of the new monetary policy tools gaining traction in the central banking community. The Bank of Japan was the first major central bank to implement YCC when it announced in 2016 that it would anchor the yield of the 10-year Japanese Government Bond (JGB) to around 0%. Interestingly, the BOJ announced YCC not to keep interest rates low but to raise them. Before YCC, the 10-year JGB was trading around -0.5%. The BOJ hoped that by raising the 10-year yield, the JGB interest-rate curve would steepen and encourage the commercial banks to lend. The BOJ has been successful in implementing YCC, with JGB yields staying within a narrow band around 0% since the announcement.

In early 2020, the Reserve Bank of Australia (RBA) became the second major central bank to implement YCC. The RBA announced that it would peg the yields of the 3-year Australian government bond to 0.25%. The announcement alone was sufficient to move the 3-year interest rates to 0.25%. The intention of the policy was to stimulate the economy through lower rates, as many of Australia's mortgages and corporate debt are around the 3-year tenor. The RBA was able to implement this target with little more than an announcement.

Does Lowering Interest Rates Really Work?

Modern central banking dogma dictates that lower interest rates can spur economic growth, which is why central banks are so eager to lower rates during a recession. However, the evidence suggests that interest rates and economic growth are not negatively correlated but positively correlated, so interest rates tend to increase along with economic growth.[71] This may in part explain why low (and even negative) interest rates in many advanced economies for the past decade failed to produce meaningful economic growth.

Suppose there were no central bank. When the economy is booming and optimism abounds, then there is a strong demand for loans. People feel confident about the future and they want to borrow money, even if interest rates are high. This increased demand for money leads to higher interest rates. On the other hand, when

---

[71] Lee, Kang-Soek, and Richard A. Werner. "Reconsidering Monetary Policy: An Empirical Examination of the Relationship Between Interest Rates and Nominal GDP Growth in the U.S., U.K., Germany and Japan." *Ecological Economics* 146 (April 2018): 26–34. https://doi.org/10.1016/j.ecolecon.2017.08.013.

economic storms are brewing and people don't feel confident about the future, then they don't borrow. They try to pay down their loans in anticipation of harder times. As demand for money declines, so do interest rates. Even without the Fed, interest rates would still follow the business cycle.

The Fed controls short-term interest rates, and it influences longer-term interest rates. Borrowers usually save a little money on their business loans or mortgage loans when the Fed lowers rates. A business or consumer may take out a loan at a 4% interest rate that they would not have taken out at 6%. But would they have taken out a loan at 2% that they would not have taken out at 3%? Even if lowering rates stimulates the economy, it likely has diminishing effects.

Taking low interest rates to the next level, Japan and the Eurozone faithfully followed their economic models and took their interest rates to negative territory. Economists at the ECB believe that negative rates encourage growth by forcing companies to invest rather than see their money disappear via negative interest rates.[72] In a sense, negative rates are like a tax on cash that is designed to force spending. Notwithstanding the research

---

[72] Altavilla, Carlo, Lorenzo Burlon, Mariassunta Giannetti, and Sarah Holton. "Is There a Zero Lower Bound? The Effects of Negative Policy Rates on Banks and Firms." Working Paper No. 2289. European Central Bank, June 2019. https://www.ecb.europa.eu/pub/pdf/scpwps/ecb.wp2289~1a3c04db25.en.pdf.

out of the ECB, the Eurozone economy has had poor growth for many years.

Negative interest rates appear to have a negative impact on bank profitability. Negative interest rates are implemented on central bank reserves, so in aggregate, it reduces the income of the banking sector. It also shifts the entire interest-rate curve lower, so loans earn less interest. Notably, European banks have been suffering declining stock prices for over ten years, while U.S. banks have been able to exceed their 2008 highs. The negative impact on the banking sector is one of the reasons U.S. policy makers are hesitant to implement negative rates. A healthy banking sector is needed to create loans that fund economic growth.

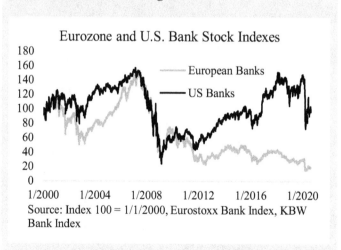

Eurozone and U.S. Bank Stock Indexes

Source: Index 100 = 1/1/2000, Eurostoxx Bank Index, KBW Bank Index

However, low or negative short-term interest rates can have tremendous impact on financial assets. This is because many speculators buy financial assets using very short-term loans. When the Fed lowers overnight rates by 1%, that fully flows through to overnight repo rates and stock market margin interest rates. Suppose an investor had bought $1 million in bonds yielding 3% interest using a repo loan at 2%. Then a decline of short-term rates of 1% would cut their interest expenses by 50% and significantly widen their interest margin. They would now even be willing to purchase bonds at lower yields (thus higher bond prices) since their interest expenses have been lowered.

Judging from a decade of experience, lower interest rates appear to boost financial assets, but not necessarily real economic growth.

Chapter 9 — How to Fed Watch

The huge impact Fed decisions have on the markets has led to the growth of a cottage industry of "Fed Watchers." These people, often holding the title of Strategist or Economist, tend to be people who worked for a few years at the Fed and then decided to double their income by joining an investment bank. They spend their time analyzing Fed actions and then share their analysis with wealthy clients or large institutional investors. They will also go on CNBC or Bloomberg and speculate on future Fed actions. Sometimes they have good insights, but most of the work they do can be done by anyone with the right information and training. This chapter will teach you the basics of Fed Watching.

Prior to the 2008 Financial Crisis, Fed actions were very opaque. In fact, sometimes the market would be surprised by the Fed's interest-rate decisions. This rarely happens anymore; the market now anticipates Fed actions accurately. This is due to the Fed's effort to improve transparency by sharing its thinking with the market. The basics of being a Fed Watcher are keeping on top of what the Fed is currently thinking, and then predicting how the Fed will behave in the future. The sections below will review the channels the Fed uses to communicate with the market.

Fed Communication and Importance	
FOMC Statement	High
FOMC Press Conference	High
FOMC Minutes	High
FOMC "Dot Plot"	High
Fed Official Speeches	Moderate
Fed Interviews	Moderate
Desk Operating Statements	Moderate
Fed Balance Sheet	Moderate
Fed Research	Low
Fed Surveys	Low

FOMC Statement

The Federal Open Market Committee (FOMC) releases a statement at the conclusion of each its meeting. The statement briefly summarizes the FOMC's view on the state of the economy and the actions the FOMC is taking to achieve its dual mandate. While no more than a page in length, the FOMC statement is very, very carefully worded to convey a precise message. Market commentators will compare current and previous statements to gauge changes in the committee's view from slight changes in wording. Declassified FOMC materials illustrate just how much thought goes into the brief statement.

The table on the following page comes from the Tealbook B prepared for the January 2014 FOMC meeting. Tealbook B, officially titled "Monetary Policy: Strategies and Alternatives" is a briefing prepared for each meeting that presents the committee with sets of policy options. The briefing is highly classified but is declassified to the public several years after publication. From the declassified briefing, you can see that the FOMC was presented with different options varying in their degree of dovishness, like a choose your own adventure script. The options show a high degree of nuance in how the Fed can proceed. With respect to language, the different choices express different degrees of optimism in the economy. With respect to balance sheet policies, the options show different degrees of accommodation by adjusting the pace of Fed QE. With respect to the funds rate, the options express very subtle differences in how soon the Fed may raise rates.

At each meeting, the FOMC will review the current briefing, discuss their view of the economy, and then vote on which courses of action to undertake.

Table 1: Overview of Policy Alternatives for January FOMC Statement

Selected Elements	December Statement	January Alternatives		
		A	**B**	**C**
Economic Conditions, Outlook, and Risks				
Economic Conditions	economic activity is expanding at a moderate pace	growth in economic activity picked up in recent quarters		
	labor market conditions have shown further improvement	labor market indicators were mixed		unchanged
	the unemployment rate has declined but remains elevated	the unemployment rate declined but remains elevated		the unemployment rate, though still elevated relative to levels judged consistent with dual mandate over the longer-run, continued to decline
	fiscal policy is restraining growth, although the extent of restraint may be diminishing	fiscal policy is restraining growth, although extent of restraint is diminishing		extent to which fiscal policy is restraining growth is diminishing
	inflation has been running below the longer-run objective	inflation has been running **well** below objective	unchanged	
Outlook	economic growth will pick up; unemployment rate will gradually decline	economic activity will expand at a moderate pace; unemployment rate will gradually decline		
Risks	risks have become more nearly balanced	risks nearly balanced but still tilted slightly to the downside	risks nearly balanced	
Balance Sheet Policies				
Agency MBS	$35 billion/month	unchanged	$30 billion/month	$25 billion/month
Treasuries	$40 billion/month	unchanged	$35 billion/month	$30 billion/month
Rationale for Purchases	cumulative progress toward maximum employment and improvement in outlook for labor market	information received about labor market and inflation does not warrant a reduction in pace	unchanged	continuing progress toward maximum employment and outlook for ongoing improvement in labor mkt
Purchase Guidance	if incoming information broadly supports expectations, will likely reduce pace in further measured steps at future meetings . . .	. . . will likely reduce pace **in measured steps** at future meetings . . .	unchanged	. . . will likely **continue to reduce pace** at future meetings . . .
Federal Funds Rate				
Target	0 to ¼ percent	unchanged		
Rate Guidance	at least as long as thresholds (6½ percent; 2½ percent) are not crossed and inflation expectations remain well anchored	unchanged		
	anticipates it likely will be appropriate to maintain current target for FFR well past time that unemployment threshold is crossed, especially if projected inflation continues to run below 2 percent	likely will be appropriate to maintain current target for FFR at least until the unemployment rate declines below [6 percent especially if] 5½ percent so long as] projected inflation continues below 2 percent	**continues to** anticipate it likely will be appropriate to maintain current target for FFR well past time that unemployment threshold is crossed . . .	unchanged
	when begin to remove accommodation, will take balanced approach	when **eventually** begin to remove accommodation, will take balanced approach	unchanged	

FOMC Press Conference

Each FOMC meeting ends with a one-hour press conference starting at 2:30 p.m. EST where the Fed Chair takes questions from the press. These press conferences are one of the most important points of Fed communication. Here, the Fed Chair is asked about a wide range of topics and the market receives their most up-to-date thinking on them. More importantly, this is on-the-fly speech that is not heavily edited and reviewed like other FOMC communications. The market watches the Chair's reactions and parses their words to guess future Fed actions. The Fed Chair also knows this is an opportunity to guide the markets, so may purposefully choose their words.

As discussed in the previous chapter, Chair Powell noted in his June 2020 FOMC press conference that he was not just not going to raise rates, but that he was "not even thinking about thinking about raising rates." With the prospect of a deep recession looming, the Chair used the opportunity to signal to the market that rates would be at zero for a very long time. Recall, the Fed controls short-term interest rates but only influences longer-term interest rates. The Chair was conducting money policy by attempting to push longer-term interest rates lower by telling the market that short-term interest rates would remain low for a long time. He wanted the market to not price in any rate hikes for a long time.

FOMC Minutes

The minutes for each FOMC meeting are released three weeks after the meeting takes place. The minutes offer a glimpse of what information was presented to the FOMC and what they discussed during the meeting. While FOMC statements are succinct, the minutes are usually around ten pages. Like the statement, the minutes are very carefully crafted to convey a specific message and the market's reaction to them is carefully monitored.

The first part of the minutes reviews the economic and financial conditions of the intermeeting period, then there is a forecast of economic conditions, and finally, there is a segment where FOMC participants discuss their views. The first two segments are put together by the Desk and Federal Reserve Board staff. The review of intermeeting period developments will largely be factual, but the Board's economic outlook is useful in informing future Fed actions. A downbeat assessment suggests a more accommodative policy.

Despite receiving a briefing on economic conditions at the meeting, each FOMC participant also has their own staff of economists and may have a different viewpoint based on the data they see in their respective district. The minutes will reveal some of the discussions that took place during the meeting but in an anonymized fashion. This will give the reader a sense as to the overall viewpoints held by FOMC participants by quantifying support for each viewpoint with words such as "majority" or "a number" or "a couple." Remember, every word in the minutes is carefully drafted and goes through many levels of review so that the intended message is communicated.

For example, the July 2020 FOMC minutes noted:

"A **majority** of participants commented on yield caps and targets—approaches that cap or target interest rates along the yield curve—as a monetary policy tool. Of those participants who discussed this option, **most** judged that yield caps and targets would likely provide only modest benefits in the current environment, as the Committee's forward guidance regarding the path of the federal funds rate already appeared highly credible and longer-term interest rates were already low. **Many** of these participants also pointed to potential costs associated with yield caps and targets."[73]

This segment was crafted to offer the reader a sense of how strongly yield curve control was supported within the FOMC. Yield curve control had been frequently discussed by FOMC members in the earlier months, but the minutes revealed that FOMC support was not strong. Treasury yields rose after the minutes were announced, suggesting that some market participants adjusted their bets after this new information.

The minutes often foreshadow policy moves in coming months. For example, in January 2018, the FOMC Minutes showed discussion of a "technical adjustment" on the interest paid on bank reserves to control the federal funds market. That technical adjustment was not discussed at the press conference at the time but was later implemented. The minutes for the April 2020 FOMC meeting contained a discussion on raising the interest rate on Fed repo loans. That was also not

---

[73] "Minutes of the Federal Open Market Committee, July 28-29, 2020." Board of Governors of the Federal Reserve System, August 19, 2020. https://www.federalreserve.gov/monetarypolicy/files/fomcminutes20200729.pdf. (Emphasis added.)

discussed at the press conference at the time but was later implemented. Fed Watchers had noticed these clues in the minutes and were expecting the actions before they took place.

FOMC "Dot Plot"

Starting in late 2007, the Fed began releasing a set of economic projections ("Summary of Economic Projections") every quarter at the March, June, September, and December FOMC meetings. The summary included projections on real economic growth, inflation, and the unemployment rate. Later in 2012, the Fed added projections for where the federal funds rate would be. Each FOMC participant's projection appears in the form of a dot of where the participant believes the appropriate policy target range would be at year-end of the specified year. The graph of the projections ends up looking like a plot of dots.

The "dot plot" is a market-moving data release because it gives a glimpse of what the trajectory of future policy rates could be and how dispersed the views are of FOMC participants. This is more concrete than the economic forecasts because it translates the forecasts into interest-rate adjustments. The more consensus there is in the dot plot, the more strongly the market will price in upcoming Fed action. But the dot plot is not always a good forecast of what will happen.

In December of 2018, the Fed's dot plot showed that a plurality of FOMC member were penciling in three 0.25% rate hikes in 2019. The target range for year-end 2018 was 2.25% to 2.5%, and the dot plot showed a plurality of FOMC participants expected the target range at year-end 2019 to be 3% to 3.25%. Furthermore, there appeared to be widespread consensus on the FOMC that at least two hikes were needed. After digesting the news, the stock market panicked and dropped to multi-year lows in the following weeks. Thereafter, the FOMC promptly did a complete roundabout in January and announced that they would be cutting rates in 2019. The stock market then strongly rebounded in the following months. When financial conditions change, the Fed can also quickly change its mind.

For release at 2:00 p.m., EST, December 19, 2018

Figure 2. FOMC participants' assessments of appropriate monetary policy: Midpoint of target range or target level for the federal funds rate

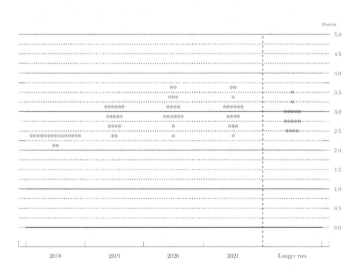

Federal Reserve Speeches

Federal Reserve Bank Presidents and Federal Reserve Board Governors routinely give speeches on how they are thinking about monetary policy.[74] They don't always agree, and some of them are much more important than others.

The voting body of the FOMC is composed of the Board Governors, the President of the New York Fed, and a set of four Presidents from the regional Federal Reserve Banks that rotates annually. Within the FOMC, the most influential people are the Chair, the Vice Chair, and the President of the New York Fed (who is also a Vice Chair). These three are called the "troika" and have the most power on the FOMC, so their thoughts must be given the most weight. In 2019, New York Fed President John Williams gave a speech suggesting that when interest rates are low, the Fed has less ammunition to combat recessions, so it should cut rates more aggressively.[75] In 2020, when the COVID-19 recession arrived, the Fed did exactly that and quickly cut rates to 0%. That move had been anticipated days before by short-term interest-rate futures traders, who were no doubt attuned the William's thinking.

In November 2019, Fed Governor Lael Brainard gave a speech speculating on the usefulness of yield curve

---

[74] The St. Louis Fed has a webpage that can help you keep abreast of all the latest Fed Speak.

[75] Williams, John C. "Living Life Near the ZLB." Speech, July 18, 2019. https://www.newyork-fed.org/newsevents/speeches/2019/wil190718.

control.[76] Chair Powell has also acknowledged some discussion of yield curve control at Fed meetings. This led many Fed Watchers to assign a high probability of the Fed implementing yield curve control in the near term. The Fed is very cautious institution, so if a policy change is mentioned in a speech, then it is already being seriously discussed internally. But then, economic conditions changed as the COVID-19 panic occurred, and Treasury yields plummeted. FOMC meeting minutes then suggested that yield curve control had been placed on the backburner but could be revived later.

FOMC members are generally labeled as either "doves" or "hawks" based on the views that they reveal. Doves prefer more accommodative monetary policy, while hawks prefer less accommodative monetary policy. Some Fed Presidents are well-known for always advocating lower rates and more quantitative easing, and some are known for the opposite. Fed Watchers can review the speeches given by each Fed president to see where they stand, then look to see who will rotate to a voting position next year to guess how the FOMC may vote.

Fed Watchers take particular note when a dove turns hawkish or when a hawk turns dovish. These shifts can

---

[76] Brainard, Lael. "Federal Reserve Review of Monetary Policy Strategy, Tools, and Communications: Some Preliminary Views." Speech, November 26, 2019. https://www.federalreserve.gov/newsevents/speech/brainard20191126a.htm.

foreshadow a shift in the FOMC's actions. For example, when even a Fed president known for being dovish is pushing back on further easing, then further easing is very unlikely.

Fed Interviews and Congressional Testimonies

Fed officials generally have a preset schedule as to when they will communicate with the market. There are prescheduled FOMC meetings, industry group conferences, or other events. But they always have the option of just calling up the press and giving an unscheduled interview. Sometimes this occurs when the Fed thinks the market has misunderstood them and they want to correct the misunderstanding before it gets out of hand. If the Fed Chair or Vice Chair ever suddenly gives an unscheduled interview, then it should be taken seriously.

Ahead of the March of 2017 FOMC meeting, short-term interest-rate markets were not pricing in any Fed action despite recent positive economic data. Fed officials then came out with a series of interviews that strongly hinted at a rate hike at the March FOMC meeting.[77] Short-term interest-rate traders took heed and began pricing it in. The FOMC delivered that hike shortly after. Remember,

---

[77] Condon, Christopher, and Rich Miller. "Fed Officials Signal More Willingness to Consider March Hike." *Bloomberg*, February 28, 2017. https://www.bloomberg.com/news/articles/2017-02-28/fed-officials-signal-greater-willingness-to-consider-march-hike.

the modern era Fed doesn't want to surprise the market too much because it does not like volatility in financial asset prices.

The Fed Chair appears before Congress twice a year at the Humphrey-Hawkins hearings (also known as Monetary Policy Report). During the hearings, the Chair offers testimony on financial and economic developments as well as Fed actions. The Chair will also take questions from members of Congress. While these hearings generate significant publicity, they usually don't reveal anything new. The Chair will largely repeat things they have said during prior FOMC press briefings, and members of Congress will largely take the opportunity to grandstand.

Desk Operating Statements

The Fed buys and sells securities through the Open Markets Desk, known as the Desk. The Desk releases its operating policies and operating calendar on the Federal Reserve Bank of New York's website. This information can tell you a bit about how the Fed is thinking about the financial markets.

During the 2020 COVID-19 panic, the Desk issued a statement on March 23rd noting they would be buying an eye-popping $75 billion in Treasuries each day.[78]

---

[78] "Statement Regarding Treasury Securities and Agency Mortgage-Backed Securities Operations." Operating Policy. Federal Reserve Bank of New York, March 23, 2020.

Over time, they tapered that amount to around $80 billion a month, which is still substantial. From this information, Fed Watchers could extrapolate the amount of liquidity the Fed was pumping into the financial system and then suggest implications that may have on interest rates and stock prices. Many market commentators saw this and believed the stock market would explode higher, which it did.

In June 2020, the Desk announced it would raise the minimum offering rate of their repo lending facility from 0.1% to 0.15%. This caused Treasury bill yields to also increase slightly as market participants speculated the move would place slight upward pressure on all short-term rates. Primary dealers' bargaining position with cash lenders would weaken as rates on borrowing from the Fed, their alternative funding source, moved up from 0.1% to 0.15%. Private sector lenders would have a bit more bargaining power to demand returns greater than 0.1%.

The Desk also posts the results of their daily operations immediately after they have concluded. Throughout the day they will post the results of their repo and reverse repo operations, MBS purchases, Treasury purchases, and securities lending. Fed Watchers notice changes in these operations and infer from them changes in the markets. For example, when participation in the Desk's reverse repo operation gradually increases, that implies that money market fund investors are having trouble

---

https://www.newyorkfed.org/markets/opolicy/operating_policy_200323.

finding higher-yielding private sector investments and are thus forced to park their money at the Fed. That usually means that there is an abundance of liquidity in the financial system and suggests that money market rates will remain low for the near future.

Fed Balance Sheet

Fed Watchers have become increasingly interested in the Fed's balance sheet as that has become a bigger part of the Fed's tool kit. They want to know whether it is growing, and if so, what assets are driving the growth. They use this information to predict what may happen to the financial markets. Generally, they assume that if the Fed is expanding its balance sheet, then interest rates will move lower and the stock market will move higher. Higher participation in some credit facilities may also be an indicator of stress in some segments of the market.

The Fed publicly discloses its balance sheet weekly in the H.4, published online every Thursday afternoon. Highlights in the H.4 include the amount of bank reserves held by commercial banks, the amount of Treasury and Agency MBS securities the Fed holds, and the size of special Fed credit facilities, as well as the amount securities held on behalf of foreign official accounts.

Reserves and Securities Holdings. Reserves and securities holdings are the flip side of each other, as reserves are created to pay for the securities that the Fed purchases.

Fed Credit Facilities. In times of significant market stress, the Fed offers special credit facilities to support certain segments of the market. In the 2020 COVID-19 panic, the Fed announced the return of several 2008 Financial Crisis–era facilities and added a few new ones. The outstanding loan balances under these facilities are disclosed weekly. The degree to which these facilities are utilized helps market participants gauge the severity of market strains. For example, the outstanding balance of FX-swap trades with foreign central banks rose to almost half a trillion dollars in April. In the same period, private market FX-swap basis exploded higher and the dollar strengthened considerably. However, the FX swaps outstanding at the Fed gradually declined after April as markers of offshore dollar funding stress also receded. Taken together, this suggests that there was tremendous amount of stress in the offshore dollar funding markets during COVID-19 panic, and those stresses were solved by half a trillion dollars in Fed liquidity.

FIMA Accounts. The Fed provides banking services to the foreign official sector clients, such as foreign central banks, foreign governments, or international organizations. The Fed provides them with two main services: a collateralized "checking account" and custodial services for their securities. The collateralized "checking account" is structured as a repo transaction, where the foreign official sector clients lend money to the Fed in the form of a repo loan. In practice, it is basically a checking account collateralized by Treasury securities. Many foreign official sector clients also hold their dollar reserve in the form of Treasury securities to earn a higher return. The Fed can act as the custodian for these securities.

Many foreign official sector clients prefer to hold their dollar reserves with the Fed because it is a risk-free counterparty. However, some also hold at least a portion of their dollar reserves with commercial banks. This could be because the commercial banks provide a more comprehensive product suite and offer higher interest rates, or for diversification reasons should geopolitical risks emerge. Market participants note when those Treasury holdings decline, because that suggests that foreign central banks are selling their Treasuries and using the dollars to intervene in the currency market.

Desk Surveys

The Desk regularly surveys market participants to try to figure out what the market is thinking. The surveys go out to the primary dealers, as well as a select group of market participants that include many of the world's largest investment funds.[79] Survey questions usually

---

[79] The list of survey respondents is available on the Federal Reserve Bank of New York's website. A sample of firms include PIMCO, Citadel, Vanguard, D.E. Shaw, BlackRock, The Carlyle Group, etc.

contain a standard set of questions on expectations of the policy rate, growth, inflation, and unemployment, and then some questions that are topical. For example, when the Fed was normalizing its balance sheet, the survey contained questions on the estimated future levels of reserve balances.

The surveys are used to try to figure out what is priced into the market so the FOMC can properly calibrate their actions. While some form of market expectations is readily observable in market pricing, the distribution of the outcomes is not. For example, amidst the Covid-19 panic in early March of 2020, the Fed funds futures market implied that the FOMC would cut rates another 0.5% at the scheduled March 17th meeting right after it had cut rates by 0.5% to 1% at an unscheduled emergency meeting on March 3rd. The March 2020 survey revealed that there was an unusually high degree of dispersion in expectations, where most respondents expected a 0.5% cut at the upcoming meeting but over a quarter of respondents expected a full 1% cut to 0%. Market pricing thus reflected the median participant but hid a large left tail expectation. This information is useful because the FOMC tries not to surprise the market too much, which could result in significant volatility. In the end, the FOMC cut by 1%, delivering a dovish but not totally unexpected surprise to the market.

In another example, the January 2014 Desk surveys revealed that market participants largely expected a slight cut of $10 billion in the monthly rate of asset purchases at the upcoming meeting. With that as the baseline expectation, the FOMC determined that a policy of no cuts in the rate of purchases would be perceived as dovish, while cuts of greater than $10 billion would be perceived as hawkish. The FOMC ultimately decided to meet the market's expectations. But if it wanted to slightly surprise the market in either direction, it knew from the surveys how to do that.

The Desk survey questionnaires are publicly available on the New York Fed's website around two weeks before an upcoming FOMC meeting, and the results of the survey are publicly available about 3 weeks after the FOMC meeting. The questions can help a Fed Watcher understand what the Fed is currently interested in, and the results can help in understanding Fed policy actions.

Federal Reserve Research

Each Federal Reserve Bank has a large staff of PhD economists who regularly publish economic research either in the form of research papers or blog posts. The research published does not necessarily reflect the views of Fed officials but is rather an outlet for staff economists to share their personal views and findings. The Fed is a very large and bureaucratic organization, so it should not be surprising to see a wide range of views that sometimes conflict. Fed economists have access to significant amounts of confidential data, so their research findings offer an opportunity to learn about the latest developments in markets. It may not add much insight as to what the FOMC will do next, but following staff research is a good way to continually educate yourself. A couple noteworthy Fed outlets are the New York Fed's Liberty Street Economics blog and the Board of Governor's FEDS Notes section. In addition, the Board of Governors' semiannual Financial Stability Report is an excellent and accessible publication that provides a good overview of the state of the financial system based on the data the Fed has collected.

Federal Reserve Surveys

The Federal Reserve Banks and the Board of Governors conduct surveys to gather qualitative information on economic conditions. A couple of the more notable surveys are the Beige Book and the Senior Loan Officer Survey. These surveys are not market moving but help in understanding how the Fed is viewing the economy.

The Beige Book, published eight times a year, is a compilation of anecdotes from business leaders in each Federal Reserve district. Federal Reserve staff conduct outreach to business contacts in their district and record their findings, particularly regarding information that pertains to employment and price changes. The Beige Book complements the Fed's trove of hard data by offering narrative context as to what is happening across regions and industries.

The Senior Loan Officer Survey, published quarterly, goes out to executives at commercial banks and is aimed at helping the Fed understand changes in credit conditions. The Fed wants to know if lending standards are tightening or loosening, since the availability of credit is a key economic indicator. When banks tighten up their lending then there is less money flowing through the system, which could be a headwind for economic growth.

What Do You Think the Fed Will Do?

A Fed Watcher will have to keep on top of all the communications discussed in this chapter and then formulate a view as to what the Fed is thinking and what the Fed will do.

Carefully reviewing all Fed communication will make you an average Fed Watcher that will be fairly accurate in benign economic conditions but inaccurate in crisis times. When something serious happens, then even the Fed is in disarray. To figure out what they will do, you would also have to be aware of how the financial system works, where the system may be breaking, and what tools the Fed has available to fix them. If you understand the concepts presented throughout this book and keep on top of Fed communications, you will be well on your way to being an expert Fed Watcher.

The New Framework
On August 27, 2020, Chair Powell announced the Fed's new monetary policy framework at the annual Jackson

Hole Economic Policy Symposium.[80] The framework made two significant changes to how the Fed conducts monetary policy: average inflation targeting and asymmetry in maximum employment.

Asymmetry in Maximum Employment

Maximum employment is one of the Fed's dual mandates. To that end, the Fed's strategy statement previously noted that its policy is informed by "deviations from [employment's] maximum level." That meant that the policy rate could be raised when employment exceeded its maximum level and could be lowered when employment was below its maximum level. In its new strategy statement, the Fed now notes its policy would be informed by "assessments of the shortfalls of employment from its maximum level." This means that employment higher than the Fed's estimated maximum level would not encourage the Fed the raise its policy rate.

Chair Powell noted in his speech that this change is in part due to the difficulty in calculating the maximum level of employment, and the flattening of the Phillips curve. The Phillips curve is a concept in economics that links the unemployment rate with inflation, where a lower unemployment rate would generate higher

---

[80] "Federal Open Market Committee Announces Approval of Updates to Its Statement on Longer-Run Goals and Monetary Policy Strategy." Press Release. Board of Governors of the Federal Reserve System, August 27, 2020. https://www.federalreserve.gov/newsevents/pressreleases/monetary20200827a.htm.

inflation. Specifically, inflation would rise when the economy exceeded its maximum employment. However, in recent years, the link between unemployment and inflation seems to have significantly weakened. Unemployment in 2019 fell to multi-decade lows of around 3.5%, yet inflation continued to be below 2%.

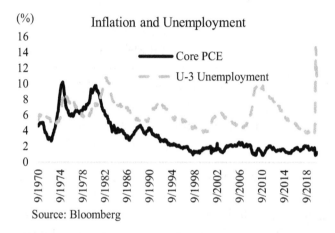

Source: Bloomberg

This puzzle suggests either that the maximum level of employment is higher than the Fed estimates or that the link between employment and inflation has changed. In either case, the Fed cannot operate on the same framework it has previously used when looking at employment data. Hence, the Fed is now saying that a low unemployment rate (high levels of employment) will no longer factor into its decision in tightening monetary policy.

Average Inflation Targeting

The Fed's second mandate is to maintain stable prices, which has been interpreted as an inflation target of 2% on the Personal Consumption Expenditures (PCE) index. For most of the past decade, the PCE was comfortably below the Fed's target. This persistent underperformance has led the Fed to change the way it implements its mandate.

The Fed has officially adopted an average inflation targeting framework where past undershoots of its inflation target would be met with future overshoots, such that the average inflation over a period of time would be around 2%. This opens the door to the Fed allowing persistent prints of inflation over 2%, which would not have been allowed under the prior framework.

Critics note that the Fed has not been able to meet its 2% inflation target for the past several years, so it is unlikely to move inflation to an even higher level to compensate for prior shortfalls. Yet, PCE inflation did occasionally exceed 2% even as the Fed hiked rates several times. If the Fed had not hiked rates at all, inflation may have persisted at levels exceeding 2%. The verdict on the effectiveness of the Fed's new framework won't become clear for another few years, but the bond market seemed to offer some degree of confidence in the Fed. After the new framework announced, the Treasury yield curve steepened, suggesting that at least some market participants anticipate higher inflation in the future.

Inflation is largely a political choice. Any government can create inflation with massive fiscal spending, and any government can create deflation by massively raising taxes. The Fed has made the choice of keeping interest rates low for a long time; should the Federal government decide to continue massive deficit spending, then the chances of higher inflation in the future are very good.

Modern Monetary Theory

Modern Monetary Theory ("MMT") is an ascendent school of economic thought that is laying the theoretical framework for a revolution in fiscal policy.[81] MMT postulates that a government issuer of fiat currency is not constrained by taxation or debt, but only by inflation. Taxation and debt issuance are merely tools through which the government manages inflation. This is in stark contrast to economic orthodoxy, which tends to negatively view deficit spending and high government debt levels.

Conventional economic thinking views a country like a household, where living beyond one's means and going into debt means leaner times ahead. A country with a high debt load would have to increase taxes on future generations to repay the debt. Too much debt may also lead investors to demand higher interest rates, further dampening economic growth. Adherents to this school of thought caution against government deficits and strive for a balanced budget.

---

[81] For more information, see Kelton, Stephanie. *The Deficit Myth: Modern Monetary Theory and the Birth of the People's Economy.* (2020)

Proponents of MMT note that the government can simply print more money to fund its spending. The government does not need to borrow or to tax, but it should use those tools to combat inflation. When the government engages in deficit spending it is actually boosting economic growth by creating money and spending it on goods and services. Deficit spending and high debt loads are not a source of concern and can be good for the economy, provided inflation is under control.

Consciously or coincidentally, the MMT revolution appears to have quietly taken over the world. Governments across the world are becoming more and more aggressive in fiscal spending and less concerned of sovereign debt loads. The U.S. deficit has gone parabolic and is running at over $3 trillion in 2020. Central banks have made this revolution possible by keeping interest rates low and funding government spending by purchasing large quantities of government debt. The economy has responded positively to the massive fiscal stimulus. More importantly, there appears to be no consequence to this behavior, as inflation remains subdued, interest rates remain historically low and currency markets remain stable. The bond vigilantes that fiscal hawks feared appear to be fairy tales.

MMT is largely correct in describing how the monetary system works, but they may have misunderstood the purpose of the bond vigilante fairy tale. A government budget is a constraint on government power, like the Bill of Rights, the separation of powers, and the

Constitution. To remove that constraint grants the government unlimited spending powers, which may or may not be wisely used.

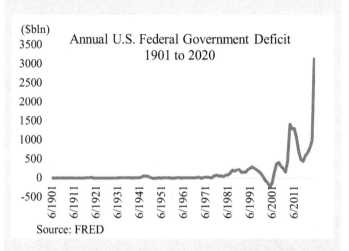

History shows over and over again that government officials are neither wiser nor less self-interested than any other person. A monetary system is only as strong as the confidence placed in it, and removing long held safeguards built into the monetary system opens up the potential for great disaster.